DOVER · THRIFT · EDITIONS

The Analects

CONFUCIUS

DOVER PUBLICATIONS, INC.
New York

DOVER THRIFT EDITIONS

General Editor: Stanley Appelbaum
Editor of This Volume: Thomas Crofts

Copyright

Published in Canada by General Publishing Company, Ltd., 30 Lesmill Road, Don Mills, Toronto, Ontario.

Bibliographical Note

This Dover edition, first published in 1995, is an unabridged republication of the translation, chronology and notes by William Edward Soothill, originally published by Oliphant, Anderson, & Ferrier, Edinburgh, 1910. For the present edition, Professor Soothill's end-notes have been arranged as footnotes. As well, a new introductory Note and two new footnotes have been specially prepared.

Library of Congress Cataloging-in-Publication Data

Confucius.
[Lun yü. English]
The Analects / translation from the Chinese by William Edward Soothill.
p. cm.
Originally published: Oliphant, Anderson, & Ferrier, Edinburgh, 1910.
ISBN 0-486-28484-0 (pbk.)
I. Soothill, William Edward, 1861–1935. II. Title.
PL2478.L7 1995
181′.112—dc20 94–24742
CIP

Manufactured in the United States of America
Dover Publications, Inc., 31 East 2nd Street, Mineola, N.Y. 11501

NOTE

Confucius (or K'ung-fu-tzu, "Master K'ung"), who lived from 551 to 479 B.C., was a philosopher, teacher and (somewhat frustrated) social reformer. Unable to secure a position in government that would allow him to put his theories into practice, he devoted himself to passing his ideas on to the next generation. He had many disciples, several of whom went on to become highly placed government officials.

The Analects (or *Lun yü*), one of the Classics of the Confucian canon, contains the conversations and sayings of Confucius, as well as observations about the Master himself, as recorded by his disciples. It pertains to political, social and personal matters, and outlines the ideal behavior of "the superior man." Lessons in *The Analects* also treat of "nobility," "Heaven," "the Golden Mean," "the correction of terms" and "virtue."

NOTE: The footnotes in this book, which with two exceptions (pp. 4 and 8, in brackets) are Professor Soothill's, very often point out repetitions, historical parallels and narrative connections between passages in the text. Both the footnotes and the index refer to books and chapters within *The Analects* by small-capital Roman numerals (for the book) and lower-case Roman numerals (for the chapter). When individual "verses" within chapters are mentioned, they are referred to by the Arabic numeral designating them in the text.

CONTENTS

VOLUME VI

VOLUME VII

VOLUME VIII

VOLUME IX

VOLUME X

CHRONOLOGY

B.C.

c. 2356. Emperor Yao, and

2255. Emperor Shun, the two great, good, semi-mythical first rulers.

2205. The Hsia Dynasty.

1766. The Shang, or Yin Dynasty.

1122. The Chou Dynasty, founded by King Wu, son of King Wên, to both of whom Confucius looked back as heroes. King Wu established the baronial fiefs, however, and in three centuries the Empire was reduced to a band of warring states.

800–729. Chêng K'ao Fu, Ancestor of Confucius.

710. Murder of his son, with whom the name K'ung began. His great-grandson moved from Sung State to Lu.

c. 625–549. Shu Liang Ho, Father of Confucius.

551. BIRTH OF CONFUCIUS.

549. Death of his Father.

532. Married. Obtained office.

530. Began teaching.

529. Death of his Mother.

523. Studied music.

518. Heir of Mêng became his pupil. Probably visited the Capital and may have met Laotzŭ.

517. Followed his Duke into exile at Ch'i, for eight years.

516. Returned to Lu. Fifteen years out of office, but teaching.

509. Duke Chao died in exile. Duke Ting succeeded.

501. Became Magistrate of Chung Tu.

500. Minister of Crime, or Chief Justice.

498. Possibly Prime Minister.

496. Present of singing-girls to Duke Ting, who accepted.

CONFUCIUS WENT INTO THIRTEEN YEARS' EXILE.

495. In Wei. Attacked in K'uang, on way to Sung.
494. In Ch'en three years.
492. Back to Wei. To Yellow River, and Chin.
491. To Ts'ai. In distress and starvation on the way.
490. In Ts'ai.
489. In Shê, and Ch'u.
488. Back to Wei, Duke Ling had died, and the state was in confusion.
485. Death of Confucius's wife.
483. RECALLED TO LU IN HIS 68TH YEAR.
482. Death of his son, Po Yü.
481. Death of Yen Hui, the beloved scholarly disciple.
480. Death of Tzŭ Lu, the bold disciple, in battle.
479. DEATH OF CONFUCIUS.
372–289. MENCIUS.

THE 36 DISCIPLES[1]

1. Ch'ên K'ang, called usually *Tzŭ Ch'in*. When his brother died, the wife and steward proposed to immolate some living persons to serve him in the shades. Tzŭ K'ang suggested none were better fitted than the wife and steward! No more was heard of the matter.
2. *Ch'i-tiao K'ai* pleased the Master for his modesty, V. v.
3. Ch'in Chang, or *Lao*. Nothing known of him except IX. vi.
4. Chung Yu, mostly called *Tzŭ Lu*, a famous disciple, like Peter for boldness, rashness, and honesty: a soldier by training and preferring his 'long sword' to all else till his Master won him to education. Confucius often smiles at his remarks. He died in battle rather than desert his feudal lord.
5. Chü Yüan, called *Chü Po Yü*, an officer in Wei who had lodged the Master during the exile and become a disciple.
6. Fan Hsü, or *Fan Ch'ih*, a young soldier, who drove the Master's chariot at times and questioned him.
7. Fu-Pu Ch'i, called *Tzŭ Chien*, who succeeded in bringing good administration to a township by considering men as men, not only labourers.
8. *Jan Ch'iu*, or Tzu Yu, or just Ch'iu, whom Confucius calls 'a man of much proficiency' and who was the means of his recall to Lu: but who gave way to the greed and military desires of Duke Ai and the Minister, Chi K'ang Tzŭ, and won the Master's disapproval on several occasions.
9. Jan Kêng, or *Po Niu*, appointed to govern Chung Tu, formerly

[1] The name in italics is that which is most used in *The Analects*, and under which name the disciple can be found in the Index to this book.

governed by Confucius, through the influence of Confucius himself.

10. Jan Yung, called *Chung Kung*, a fine character, though his father was noted for his meanness, VI. iv. Kinsman to the two preceding.
11. *Ju Pei*, a former disciple who had given offence, and whom the Master refused to receive, XVII. xx.
12. Kao Ch'ai, or *Tzŭ Kao*, 'dwarfish and ugly, but of great worth and ability'. Tzŭ Lu had him appointed the Governor of Pi, a border town, XI. xxiv.
13. *Kung-hsi Ch'ih*, or Tzŭ Hua or Ch'ih: noted for his knowledge of the Rites.
14. *Kung-yeh Ch'ang*, who had been wrongfully imprisoned; a good man to whom Confucius gave his daughter as wife.
15. *Kung-po Liao*, known only for his slandering Tzü Lu.
16. K'ung Li, or *Po Yü*, son of Confucius.
17. *Lin Fang*: all that is known of him is in III. iv and vi.
18. Min Sun, or *Min Tzŭ Ch'ien*, noted for purity and filial affection.
19. *Nan-kung Kua*, or Nan Yung, to whom Confucius gave his elder brother's daughter as wife. When the palace of Duke Ai was on fire, and others thought only of saving goods, he saved the library, thus preserving the Annals of the Chou Dynasty, and other antiquities.
20. Pu Shang, or *Tzŭ Hsia*. When his son died he nearly wept himself blind, but lived to a great age, and presented copies of the Classics to Prince Wên of Wei in 406 B.C. An exact scholar, but lacking width of scholarship.
21. *Shên Ch'êng* has left no trace, except that he was strong and passionate, V. ix.
22. *Ssŭ-ma Kêng*, brother of the bad official Huan Ti who tried to have Confucius killed.
23. *Tan-t'ai Mieh-ming*, so ugly that at first Confucius was repelled. Later he had three hundred disciples, and his memory is revered still in Kiangsu, VI. xii.
24. Tsai Yü, or Tzŭ Wo, or *Tsai Wo*, took part in a rising which caused Confucius to be ashamed of him: argues several times with the Master; a cynic.
25. Tsêng Shên, or *Tsêng Tzŭ*, or Shên, as Confucius sometimes calls him, is one of the most famous disciples. Of wide learning,

pleasing in appearance, noble and dignified, solid in virtue, and of impressive speech: so says Tzŭ Kung. His love for his parents was phenomenal. As a boy, gathering fuel on the hills, he once realized that his mother needed him greatly. She had bitten her finger, to call him, in default of other means, and he felt the pain! Every time he read the mourning rites, he was moved to tears. He composed the Classic of Filial Piety, probably under Confucius's direction, edited the Great Learning, and may have composed ten books of the Book of Rites.

26. *Tsên Tien*, father of Tsêng Tzŭ, who loved peaceful joys, V. xxiv.
27. *Tso-ch'iu Ming* is considered rather a predecessor than a disciple of the Sage, though his tablet is with the disciples in the temples, V. xxiv.
28. Tuan-mu Tzŭ, or *Tzŭ Kung*, a fine disciple, said to have risen from poverty to affluence through his abilities, and of such diplomatic talents that tradition says he saved the state of Lu from the machinations of the more powerful state of Ch'i. He was so devoted to the Master that he remained at his grave three years with the other disciples, and three years after that.
29. Tuan-sun Shih, or *Tzŭ Chang*, noted for his humility and diligence.
30. *Tzu-fu Ching-po*, an officer of Lu, of whom little is known.
31. *Wu-ma Shih*, thirty years younger than Confucius, but little known.
32. *Yen Hui*, or Yen Yüan, Tzŭ Yüan, or often called Hui by Confucius, the beloved disciple, an unostentatious scholar, white-haired at 29 through hard study. Confucius bewailed him so much at his death that the disciples remonstrated.
33. *Yen Wu Yao*, father of Yen Yüan, and of poor family circumstances.
34. Yen Yen, or *Tzŭ Yu*, distinguished for his literary acquirements. He reformed the people of Wu Ch'êng by civilizing arts, and was commended by the Master.
35. Yu Jo, or *Tzŭ Yu*, but later known as the philosopher Yu Tzŭ, was noted for his good memory and love of antiquity. He resembled in voice and appearance the Master so closely that, when Confucius died, the disciples proposed to put him in Confucius' place. Along with the disciples of Tsêng Tzŭ, his followers are credited with the compilation of *The Analects*.
36. Yüan Hsien, or *Yüan Ssŭ*, noted for his purity of purpose, modesty, and happiness despite poverty.

NOTE ON THE CONVERSATIONS

CONFUCIUS is said always to have answered the questions of his disciples according to their character and need.

Thus it is told, for instance, when Tzŭ Lu the soldier first sought him, Confucius asked him of what he was most fond. 'My long sword!' replied Tzŭ Lu. Confucius suggested that if he added culture to his present ability, he would be a more superior man. Tzŭ Lu replied: 'On the southern hill is a bamboo, straight by nature and that needs no bending: if you cut it down and use it, it will pierce the hide of a rhinoceros. What need is there of learning?' Replied the Master: 'Yes, but if you notch and feather it, barb and sharpen it, will it not penetrate much deeper?' Tzŭ Lu understood, and willingly submitted to be taught.

DRAMATIS PERSONAE

CONFUCIUS, called THE MASTER usually, but sometimes referred to by his official name of CHUNG NI, or the MASTER K'UNG. Usually called CH'IU when he speaks of himself.

His 36 Disciples: 'The ten discerning ones' are his main interlocutors, though all take some share.

References are made to:

Duke Ling of Wei, with his beautiful dissolute wife, Nan-Tzŭ.

Duke Ting of Lu, whose acceptance of the 80 courtesans drove Confucius out of the State of Lu.

Duke Ai of Lu, who reigned when Confucius was recalled to Lu.

Duke of Shê, a very small state, who had arrogated to himself the title.

Duke Ching of Ch'i, who was too old to reform.

Various Ministers of State, chief of whom are:

Chi K'ang Tzu, who recalled first Jan Ch'iu, then the disciples, from exile, and later Confucius. An inquirer as to good government, but not a very good practiser.

Huan T'ui, brother of a disciple, but who had tried to have Confucius killed by a falling tree during the exile.

VOLUME I

BOOK I

Concerning Fundamental Principles

CHAPTER I

1. The Master said: 'Is it not indeed a pleasure to acquire knowledge and constantly to exercise oneself therein? 2. And is it not delightful to have men of kindred spirit come to one from afar? 3. But is not he a true philosopher who, though he be unrecognized of men, cherishes no resentment?'

CHAPTER II[1]

1. The philosopher Yu said: 'He who lives a filial life, respecting the elders, who yet is wishful to give offence to those above him, is rare; and there has never been any one unwishful to offend those above him, who has yet been fond of creating disorder. 2. The true philosopher devotes himself to the fundamentals, for when those have been established right courses naturally evolve; and are not filial devotion and respect for elders the very foundations of an unselfish life?'

CHAPTER III

The Master said: 'Artful speech and an ingratiating demeanour rarely accompany virtue.'

CHAPTER IV

The philosopher Tsêng said: 'I daily examine myself on three points,— In planning for others have I failed in conscientiousness? In intercourse with friends have I been insincere? And have I failed to practise what I have been taught?'

---

[1] ii. and iv. The followers of the two philosopher-disciples Yu (Tzŭ Lu) and Tsêng (Tsêng Tzŭ) are credited with compiling *The Analects*: so here they mention specially their own masters.

CHAPTER V

The Master said: 'To conduct the government of a State of a thousand chariots there must be religious attention to business and good faith, economy in expenditure and love of the people, and their employment on public works at the proper seasons.'

CHAPTER VI

The Master said: 'When a youth is at home let him be filial, when abroad respectful to his elders; let him be circumspect and truthful and, while exhibiting a comprehensive love for all men, let him ally himself with the good. Having so acted, if he have energy to spare, let him employ it in polite studies.'

CHAPTER VII

Tzŭ Hsia said: 'He who transfers his mind from feminine allurement to excelling in moral excellence; who in serving his parents is ready to do so to the utmost of his ability; who in the service of his prince is prepared to lay down his life; and who in intercourse with his friends is sincere in what he says, — though others may speak of him as uneducated, I should certainly call him educated.'

CHAPTER VIII

1. The Master said: 'A scholar who is not grave will not inspire respect, and his learning will therefore lack stability. 2. His chief principles should be conscientiousness and sincerity. 3. Let him have no friends unequal to himself. 4. And when in the wrong let him not hesitate to amend.'

CHAPTER IX

The philosopher Tsêng said: 'Solicitude on the decease of parents, and the pursuit of this for long after, would cause an abundant restoration of the people's morals.'

CHAPTER X

Tzŭ Ch'in inquired of Tzŭ Kung saying: 'When the Master arrives at any State he always hears about its administration. Does he ask for this information, or, is it tendered to him?' 2. 'The Master,' said Tzŭ Kung, 'is benign, frank, courteous, temperate, deferential and thus obtains it. The Master's way of asking,—how different it is from that of others!'

CHAPTER XI

The Master said: 'While a man's father lives, mark his tendencies; when his father is dead, mark his conduct. If for three years he does not change from his father's ways, he may be called filial.'

CHAPTER XII

1. The philosopher Yu said: 'In the usages of decorum it is naturalness that is of value. In the regulations of the ancient kings this was the admirable feature, both small and great deriving therefrom. 2. But there is a naturalness that is not permissible; for to know to be natural, and yet to be so beyond the restraints of decorum is also not permissible.'

CHAPTER XIII

The philosopher Yu said: 'When you make a promise consistent with what is right, you can keep your word. When you show respect consistent with good taste, you keep shame and disgrace at a distance. When he in whom you confide is one who does not fail his friends, you may trust him fully.'

CHAPTER XIV

The Master said: 'The scholar who in his food does not seek the gratification of his appetite, nor in his dwelling is solicitous of comfort, who is diligent in his work, and guarded in his speech, who associates with the high-principled, and thereby directs himself aright,—such a one may really be said to love learning.'

CHAPTER XV

1. 'What do you think,' asked Tzŭ Kung, 'of the man who is poor yet not servile, or who is rich yet not proud?' 'He will do,' replied the Master, 'but he is not equal to the man who is poor and yet happy, or rich and yet loves courtesy.' 2. Tzŭ Kung remarked: 'The Ode says this is

Like cutting, then filing;
Like chiselling, then grinding.

That is the meaning of your remark, is it not?' 3. 'Tz'ŭ!' said the Master. 'Now indeed I can begin to talk with him about the Odes, for when I tell him the premise he knows the conclusion.'[2]

CHAPTER XVI

The Master said: 'I will not grieve that men do not know me; I will grieve that I do not know men.'

[2] [Here and elsewhere in *The Analects* Confucius refers to *The Odes,* or *Shih Ching,* a collection of some 300 poems that constitutes one of the classics of the Confucian Canon. Confucius is said to have edited and compiled *The Odes* himself.]

BOOK II

Concerning Government

Chapter I

The Master said: 'He who governs by his moral excellence may be compared to the pole-star, which abides in its place, while all the stars bow towards it.'

Chapter II

The Master said: 'Though the Odes number three hundred, one phrase can cover them all, namely, "With purpose undiverted" '

Chapter III

1. The Master said: 'If you govern the people by laws, and keep them in order by penalties, they will avoid the penalties, yet lose their sense of shame. 2. But if you govern them by your moral excellence, and keep them in order by your dutiful conduct, they will retain their sense of shame, and also live up to this standard.'

Chapter IV

1. The Master said: 'At fifteen I set my mind upon wisdom. 2. At thirty I stood firm. 3. At forty I was free from doubts. 4. At fifty I understood the laws of Heaven. 5. At sixty my ear was docile. 6. At seventy I could follow the desires of my heart without transgressing the right.'

Chapter V

1. When Mêng I Tzŭ[1] asked what filial duty meant, the Master answered: 'It is not being disobedient.' 2. Afterwards when Fan Ch'ih was

[1] Mêng I Tzŭ, or Mêng Sun, a minister of Lu who gave orders on his death-bed, 518 B.C., that his son should be sent to Confucius. In these Chapters (v–viii) Confucius answers each inquirer differently.

driving him the Master told him, saying: 'Mêng Sun asked me what filial piety meant, and I replied "Not being disobedient."' 3. Fan Ch'ih thereupon asked, 'What did you mean?' The Master answered: 'While parents live serve them rightfully; when they are dead bury them with filial rites, and sacrifice to them with proper ordinances.'

CHAPTER VI

When Mêng Wu Po[2] asked what filial duty meant the Master answered: 'Parents should only have anxiety when their children are ill.'

CHAPTER VII

When Tzŭ Yu asked the meaning of filial piety the Master said: 'The filial piety of the present day merely means to feed one's parents; but even one's dogs and horses receive their food;—without reverence wherein lies the difference?'

CHAPTER VIII

When Tzŭ Hsia asked the meaning of filial piety the Master said: 'The behaviour is the difficult matter. When anything is to be done, then the young should undertake the burden of it; when there is wine and food, then they should serve them to their seniors. But is this alone to be considered filial piety?'

CHAPTER IX

The Master said: 'I could talk to Hui[3] for a whole day and, as if he were stupid, he never raised an objection; but when he withdrew and I examined into his conduct when not with me, I nevertheless found him fully competent to demonstrate what I had taught him. Hui! he was not stupid.'

CHAPTER X

1. The Master said: 'Observe what he does; 2. look into his motives; 3. find out in what he is at peace. 4. Can a man hide himself? Can a man hide himself?'

---

[2] Mêng Wu Po, son of Mêng I Tzŭ, above.
[3] Hui is Yen Hui, or Yen Yüan, but usually called Hui by the Master; his favourite.

CHAPTER XI

The Master said: 'He who keeps on reviewing his old and acquiring new knowledge may become a teacher of others.'

CHAPTER XII

The Master said: 'The higher type of man is not a machine.'

CHAPTER XIII

On Tzŭ Kung asking about the nobler type of man the Master said: 'He first practises what he preaches and afterwards preaches according to his practice.'

CHAPTER XIV

The Master said: 'The nobler type of man is broad-minded and not prejudiced. The inferior man is prejudiced and not broad-minded.'

CHAPTER XV

The Master said: 'Learning without thinking is useless. Thinking without learning is dangerous.'

CHAPTER XVI

The Master said: 'To devote oneself to irregular speculations is decidedly harmful.'

CHAPTER XVII

The Master said: 'Yu![4] Shall I teach you the meaning of knowledge? When you know a thing to recognize that you know it; and when you do not, to know that you do not know,—that is knowledge.'

CHAPTER XVIII

1. Tzŭ Chang was studying with a view to preferment. 2. The Master said to him: 'Hear much, be reserved in what causes you doubt, and

[4] Yu was bold Tzŭ Lu's personal name.

speak guardedly of the rest; you will then suffer little criticism. See much, be reserved in what seems imprudent, and act guardedly as to the rest; you will then have few regrets. With little for criticism in your speech, and little to regret in your conduct, — herein you will find preferment.'

Chapter XIX

Duke Ai[5] inquired saying: 'What should I do to insure the contentment of the people?' 'If you promote the upright and dismiss the ill-doer,' replied Confucius, 'the people will be contented; but if you promote the ill-doer and dismiss the upright, the people will be discontented.'

Chapter XX

When Chi K'ang Tzŭ[6] asked how to inspire the people with respect and loyalty, so that they might be mutually emulous (for the welfare of the state), the Master said: 'Lead them with dignity and they will also be dutiful; be filial and kind and they will be loyal; promote those who excel and teach the incompetent, and they will encourage each other.'

Chapter XXI

1. Some one addressed Confucius with the remark: 'Why, Sir, are you not in the public service?' 2. The Master answered: 'Does not the *Book of History*[7] say concerning filial duty, — "But one's duty as a son and friendliness to one's brethren are shown forth in the public service?" These then are also public service. Why should your idea alone be considered as constituting public service?'

Chapter XXII

The Master said: 'A man who is without good faith — I do not know how he is to manage! How can a waggon without its yoke-bar for the ox, or a carriage without its collar-bar for the horses, be made to move?'

---

[5] Duke Ai, 494–467 B.C., was duke of Lu on Confucius's return from exile.

[6] Chi K'ang Tzŭ, sometimes K'ang Tzŭ, or Chi-sun, was minister to the above: he had Confucius recalled from exile, after the disciple Jan Ch'iu had acted for some years.

[7] [The *Book of History*, or *Shû Ching*, may be the earliest extant classical Chinese text. It is a compilation of historical documents pertaining roughly to the period between 2357 and 627 B.C.; it existed in a fragmented state even in Confucius's time but was nevertheless regarded as essential reading for scholars.]

CHAPTER XXIII

1. Tzŭ Chang asked whether the condition of things ten ages hence could be foreknown. 2. The Master answered: 'The Yin dynasty perpetuated the civilization of the Hsia; its modifications and accretions can be known. The Chou perpetuated the civilization of the Yin, and its modifications and accretions can be known. Whatever others may succeed the Chou, their character, even a hundred ages hence, can be known.'

CHAPTER XXIV

1. The Master said: 'To sacrifice to a spirit of an ancestor not one's own is sycophancy. 2. To see the right and not do it is cowardice.'

VOLUME II

BOOK III

The Eight Dancers: Concerning Manners and Morals

CHAPTER I

Confucius said of the head of the House of Chi,[1] who had eight rows of dancers performing in his Temple: 'If he can bear to do this, what can he not bear to do?'

CHAPTER II

The members of the three great Houses of Lu[2] used the Yung Ode at the removal of the sacrifices. The Master said:

' "Assisted by princes and noblemen,
Solemnly stands the Son of Heaven," —
What application can this have in the hall
merely of the three Families?'

CHAPTER III

The Master said: 'A man who is not virtuous, what has he to do with worship? A man who is not virtuous, what has he to do with the music of the temple?'

CHAPTER IV

1. Lin Fang[3] asked what was the chief principle in observances of ritual. 2. The Master answered: 'A great question indeed! 3. In ceremonies in

[1] *Circ.* 515 B.C. The Chi and the Mêng families were all descendants of Duke Huan, 710 B.C., upon whom permission to use Imperial rites had been bestowed: but for a cadet family like Chi to perform them was pure arrogance.

[2] Again arrogant families usurping Imperial rites.

[3] Chapters iv. and vi. are the only occasions we hear of the disciple Lin Fang.

general, it is better to be simple than lavish: and in the rites of mourning, heart-felt distress is better than observance of detail.'

Chapter V

The Master said: 'The tribes of the east and north have their princes, and are not, like all our great land, without leaders.'

Chapter VI

When the chief of the Chi family was going to sacrifice on Mount T'ai,[4] the Master addressing Jan Yu said: 'Can you not save him from this sin?' 'I cannot,' he replied. 'Alas!' said the Master, 'is that not saying that the Spirit of Mount T'ai is not equal to that of Lin Fang?'

Chapter VII

The Master said: 'A gentleman never contends in anything he does—except perhaps in archery. Even then, he bows to his rival and yields him the way as they ascend the pavilion; in like manner he descends and offers him the penalty cup,—in his contentions he is still a gentleman.'

Chapter VIII

1. Tzŭ Hsia asked: 'What is the meaning of the passage,[5]—

"As she artfully smiles
What dimples appear!
Her bewitching eyes
Show their colours so clear.
Ground spotless and candid
For tracery splendid!"?'

2. 'The painting comes after the ground-work,' answered the Master.
3. 'Then manners are secondary?' said Tzŭ Hsia. ' 'Tis Shang[6] who unfolds my meaning,' replied the Master. 'Now indeed, I can begin to discuss the poets with him.'

---

[4] Similar usurpation, but on the summit of a sacred mountain.
[5] Quoted from one of the poems excluded by Confucius from *The Odes*.
[6] Shang was Tzŭ Hsia's personal name.

Chapter IX

The Master said: 'I can describe the civilization of the Hsia dynasty, but the descendant State of Ch'i does not yield adequate documentation. I can describe the civilization of the Yin dynasty, but the descendant State of Sung does not yield adequate documentation. And all because of the deficiency of their records and wise men. Were those sufficient, then I could confirm my views.'

Chapter X

The Master said: 'At the Quinquennial Sacrifice in the Lu Ancestral Temple, after the libation has been sprinkled, I have no further wish to look on.'[7]

Chapter XI

When some one asked the meaning of the Quinquennial Sacrifice, the Master replied: 'I do not know. He who knew its meaning, would he not find himself in regard to the whole Empire as if he were looking upon this?'—pointing to his palm.[8]

Chapter XII

1. He sacrificed to his forefathers as if they were present; he sacrificed to the gods as if the gods were present. 2. The Master said: 'For me not to be present at a sacrifice is as if I did not sacrifice.'

Chapter XIII

1. Wang-sun Chia[9] inquired: 'What is the meaning of the saying, "It is better to pay court to the god of the Hearth than to the god of the Hall"?'. 2. 'Not so,' answered Confucius, 'He who sins against Heaven has nowhere left for prayer.'

---

[7] The rest of the ceremony was usurpation.

[8] The meaning of this has been much disputed.

[9] Wang-sun Chia, an over-powerful official of Wei: and he was suggesting that it paid better to give homage to the kitchen servants than in the family temple.

Chapter XIV

The Master said: 'Chou had the advantage of surveying the two preceding dynasties. How full was its culture! I follow Chou dynasty ideas.'

Chapter XV

When the Master first entered the Grand Temple he asked about everything, whereupon some one remarked: 'Who says the son of the man of Tsou knows the correct forms? On entering the Grand Temple he asks about everything.' The Master hearing of it remarked: 'This too is correct form.'

Chapter XVI

The Master said: 'In archery piercing the target is not the essential, for men are not of equal strength. Such was the rule of yore.'

Chapter XVII

1. Tzŭ Kung wished to dispense with the live sheep presented in the Ducal Temple at the announcement of the new moon. 2. The Master said: 'T'zŭ! You care for the sheep. I care for the ritual.'

Chapter XVIII

The Master said: 'If one were to serve one's prince with perfect homage, people to-day would deem it sycophancy.'

Chapter XIX

When Duke Ting[10] asked how a prince should employ his ministers, and how ministers should serve their prince, Confucius replied saying: 'A prince should employ his ministers with courtesy. A minister should serve his prince with loyalty.'

Chapter XX

The Master said: 'The Kuan Chu Ode[11] is passionate without being sensual, is plaintive without being morbid.'

---

[10] This occurred before the exile, while Confucius was still minister in Lu to Duke Ting.

[11] The *Kuan Chu Ode* utters good King Wên's longing in ancient times for his bride.

CHAPTER XXI

1. When Duke Ai asked Tsai Wo[12] concerning the altars to the tutelary deities of the land, 2. Tsai Wo responded: 'The sovereign of Hsia adopted the pine, the men of Yin the cypress, but the men of Chou the chestnut, intimating that the people should stand in dread.' 3. On the Master hearing of this he said: 'When a deed is done it is useless to discuss it, when a thing has taken its course it is useless to remonstrate, what is past and gone it is useless to blame.'

CHAPTER XXII

1. The Master said: 'The calibre of Kuan Chung's[13] mind was but limited!' 2. Some one observed: 'Do you mean that Kuan Chung was economical?' 3. 'Kuan,' he replied, 'maintained his San Kuei palace, and the members of his staff performed no double duties, — how can he be considered economical?' 4. 'But surely Kuan Chung understood etiquette?' 5. 'The prince of a state,' said Confucius, 'has a screen to mask his gate, — Kuan too had his gate-screen. Princes of state, when two of them have a friendly meeting, use a stand for their inverted pledge-cups, — Kuan too used such a cup-stand. If Kuan understood etiquette, who does not understand it?'

CHAPTER XXIII

The Master discoursing to the state Band Master of Lu on the subject of music said: 'The art of music may be readily understood. The attack should be prompt and united, and as the piece proceeds it should do so harmoniously, with clearness of tone, and continuity of time, and so on to its conclusion.'

CHAPTER XXIV

The Officer in charge of the frontier town of I requested an interview, saying: 'Whenever a man of virtue has come here I have never failed to obtain an interview,' — whereupon the followers of the Sage introduced him. On coming out he observed: 'Why do you grieve, gentlemen, over this loss of office? The Empire for long has been without light and leading; but Heaven is now going to use your Master as an arousing tocsin.'

---

[12] The disciple Tsai Wo took part in a rebellion and earned his Master's disapproval.

[13] Kuan Chung has been called the Bismarck of ancient China. His motto was, 'I give that you may give in return.'

CHAPTER XXV

The Master spoke of the Shao[14] music as perfectly beautiful in form and perfectly good in its influence. He spoke of the Wu[15] music as perfectly beautiful in form but not perfectly good in its influence.

CHAPTER XXVI

The Master said: 'High station filled without magnanimity, religious observances performed without reverence, and "mourning" conducted without grief, — from what standpoint shall I view such ways?'

[14] *The Shao*, a piece of ancient ritual music, meaning 'The Succession to the Dynasty'.
[15] *The Wu* meant 'The Overthrow'.

BOOK IV

Concerning Virtue

Chapter I

The Master said: 'It is the moral character of a neighbourhood that constitutes its excellence, and how can he be considered wise who does not elect to dwell in moral surroundings?'

Chapter II

The Master said: 'A man without virtue cannot long abide in adversity, nor can he long abide in happiness; but the virtuous man is at rest in virtue, and the wise man covets it.'

Chapter III

The Master said: 'Only the virtuous are competent to love or to hate men.'

Chapter IV

The Master said: 'He who has really set his mind on virtue will do no evil.'

Chapter V

1. The Master said: 'Wealth and rank are what men desire, but unless they be obtained in the right way they may not be possessed. Poverty and obscurity are what men detest; but unless prosperity be brought about in the right way, they are not to be abandoned. 2. If a man of honour forsake virtue how is he to fulfil the obligations of his name? 3. A man of honour never disregards virtue, even for the space of a single meal. In moments of haste he cleaves to it; in seasons of peril he cleaves to it.'

Chapter VI

1. The Master said: 'I have never seen one who loved virtue, nor one who hated what was not virtuous. He who loved virtue would esteem nothing above it; and he who hated what is not virtuous would himself be so virtuous that he would allow nothing evil to adhere to him. 2. Is there any one able for a single day to devote his strength to virtue? I have never seen such a one whose ability would be sufficient. 3. If perchance there be such I have never seen him.'

Chapter VII

The Master said: 'A man's faults all conform to his type of mind. Observe his faults and you may know his virtues.'

Chapter VIII

The Master said: 'He who heard the truth in the morning might die content in the evening.'

Chapter IX

The Master said: 'The student who aims at wisdom, and yet who is ashamed of shabby clothes and poor food, is not yet worthy to be discoursed with.'

Chapter X

The Master said: 'The wise man in his attitude towards the world has neither predilections nor prejudices. He is on the side of what is right.'

Chapter XI

The Master said: 'The man of honour thinks of his character, the inferior man of his position. The man of honour desires justice, the inferior man favour.'

Chapter XII

The Master said: 'He who works for his own interests will arouse much animosity.'

CHAPTER XIII

The Master said: 'Is a prince able to rule his country with courtesy and deference, — then what difficulty will he have? And if he cannot rule his country with courtesy and deference, what use are the forms of courtesy to him?'

CHAPTER XIV

The Master said: 'One should not be concerned at lack of position, but should be concerned about what will fit him to occupy it. One should not be concerned at being unknown, but should seek to be worthy of being known.'

CHAPTER XV

1. The Master said: 'Shên![1] My teaching contains one all-pervading principle.' 'Yes,' replied Tsêng Tzŭ. 2. When the Master had left the room the disciples asked, 'What did he mean?' Tsêng Tzŭ replied, 'Our Master's teaching is simply this: Conscientiousness within and consideration for others.'

CHAPTER XVI

The Master said: 'The wise man is informed in what is right. The inferior man is informed in what will pay.'

CHAPTER XVII

The Master said: 'When you see a man of worth, think how to rise to his level. When you see an unworthy man, then look within and examine yourself.'

CHAPTER XVIII

The Master said: 'In his duty to his parents a son may gently remonstrate with them. If he see that they are not inclined to yield, he should be increasingly respectful but not desist, and though they deal hardly with him he must not complain.'

---

[1] Shên, surname of Tsêng Tzŭ.

CHAPTER XIX

The Master said: 'While a father or mother are alive, a son should not travel far. If he travel he must have a stated destination.'

CHAPTER XX

The Master said: 'If for three years a son does not change from his father's ways, he may be called filial.'

CHAPTER XXI

The Master said: 'The age of one's parents should ever be kept in mind, as an occasion at once for joy and for fear.'

CHAPTER XXII

The Master said: 'The men of old were reserved in speech out of shame lest they should come short in deed.'

CHAPTER XXIII

The Master said: 'The self-restrained seldom err.'

CHAPTER XXIV

The Master said: 'The wise man desires to be slow to speak but quick to act.'

CHAPTER XXV

The Master said: 'Virtue never dwells alone; it always has neighbours.'

CHAPTER XXVI

Tzŭ Yu said: 'In serving one's prince importunity results in disgrace; as importunity between friends results in estrangement.'

VOLUME III

BOOK V

Concerning Certain Disciples and Others

CHAPTER I

1. The Master said of Kung Yeh Ch'ang that he was a suitable man to marry, for though he had been in prison it was through no wrong-doing of his. So he gave him his own daughter to wife. 2. The Master said of Nan Yung[1] that when the country was well governed he would not be set aside, and when the country was ill governed he would escape suffering and death. So he gave him his elder brother's daughter to wife.

CHAPTER II

The Master said of Tzŭ Chien: 'An honourable man indeed is such a one as he! Were the state of Lu without men of honour how could he have acquired this excellence?'

CHAPTER III

Tzŭ Kung asked: 'What is your opinion of me?' 'You are a vessel,' said the Master. 'What sort of a vessel?' he asked. 'A jewelled temple-vessel' was the reply.

CHAPTER IV

1. Some one remarked: 'A virtuous man is Yung, but he is not ready of speech.' 2. 'What need has he of ready speech?' said the Master. 'The man who is always ready with his tongue to others will often be disliked by them. I do not know about his virtue, but what need has he of ready speech?'

---

[1] Kung Yeh Ch'ang and Nan Yung: two worthy disciples.

Chapter V

The Master wanted to engage Ch'i-tiao K'ai in office, but he replied: 'I still lack confidence for this.' Whereat the Master was pleased.

Chapter VI

The Master said: 'My doctrines make no progress. I will get me on a raft and float away upon the sea! If any one accompanies me will it not be Yu?' Tzŭ Lu on hearing this was pleased; whereupon the Master said: 'Yu is fonder of daring than I; he also exercises no discretion.'

Chapter VII[2]

1. Mêng Wu Po asked whether Tzŭ Lu was a man of virtue. The Master answered: 'I do not know.' 2. On his repeating the question the Master said: 'Yu! In a kingdom of a thousand chariots he might be appointed to the administration of its levies, but I do not know about his virtue.' 3. 'What about Ch'iu?' he asked, to which the Master replied: 'Ch'iu! Over a city of a thousand families, or a household of a hundred chariots, he might be appointed as controller; but I do not know about his virtue.' 4. 'And what about Ch'ih?' he asked. 'Ch'ih!' said the Master. 'Girded with his sash and standing in a Court, he might be appointed to converse with its guests; but I do not know about his virtue.'

Chapter VIII

1. The Master addressing Tzŭ Kung said: 'Which is the superior, you or Hui?' 2. 'How dare I look at Hui?' he answered; 'Hui hears one point and from it apprehends the whole ten. I hear one point and apprehend a second therefrom.' 3. The Master said: 'You are not equal to him, I grant you, you are not equal to him.'

Chapter IX

1. Tsai Yü spending the daytime in sleep, the Master said: 'Rotten wood is unfit for carving, and a wall of dirt unfit for plastering. As to Yü, — what is the use of reproving him!' 2. 'Formerly,' he continued, 'my attitude towards others was to hear what they said and give them credit for their

[2] vii–ix. Mêng Wu Po, see II. vi. Tzŭ-Lu = Yu; Jan Ch'iu = Ch'iu; Kung-hsi Ch'ih = Ch'ih; Tsai Yü, or Yü = Tsai Wo.

deeds. Now my attitude towards others is to listen to what they say and note what they do. It is through Yü that I have made this change.'

Chapter X

The Master said: 'I have never seen a man of strong character.' Some one remarked, "There is Shên Ch'êng.' 'Ch'êng!' said the Master. 'He is under the influence of his passions, and how can he be possessed of strength of character?'

Chapter XI

Tzŭ Kung said: 'What I do not wish others to do to me, that also I wish not to do to them.' "Tz'ŭ!' observed the Master, 'that is a point to which you have not attained.'

Chapter XII

Tzŭ Kung said: 'Our Master's culture and refinement all may hear; but our Master's discourse on the nature of man and the laws of heaven it is not given to all to hear.'

Chapter XIII

When Tzŭ Lu heard any precept and had not yet been able to put it into practice, he was only afraid lest he should hear some other.

Chapter XIV

Tzŭ Kung asked: 'On what ground has K'ung Wên Tzŭ received his posthumous title of Wên?' 'He was clever and fond of learning,' replied the Master, 'and he was not ashamed to seek knowledge from his inferiors;—that is why he has been styled "Cultured".'[3]

Chapter XV

The Master remarked of Tzŭ Ch'an[4] that he had four of the Ideal Man's characteristics;—in his personal conduct he was serious, in his duty to

[3] A play on the name, Wên, which means 'Cultured'. K'ung Wên Tzŭ had caused his lord to divorce his wife, and then married his own daughter first to him, and later to his successor. Yet he had desire for knowledge.

[4] A high officer of state who later wept at Confucius's death.

his superior he was deferential, in providing for the people he was beneficent, and in directing them he was just.

CHAPTER XVI

The Master said: 'Yen P'ing Chung[5] was gifted in the art of friendship. Whatever the lapse of time, he maintained towards his friends the same consideration.'

CHAPTER XVII

The Master said: 'Tsang Wên Chung[6] kept a large tortoise in an edifice, on whose pillar-tops were representations of hills, and on its king-posts of water plants, — of what sort was his wisdom?'

CHAPTER XVIII

1. Tzŭ Chang asked: 'The Prime Minister Tzŭ Wên[7] thrice took office as prime minister with never a sign of elation, and, though thrice retired from it, showed never a sign of annoyance; also he never failed to explain to the new Minister the policy of his late ministry; — what would you say of him?' 'He was conscientious,' answered the Master. 'Was he a man of ideal virtue?' asked the disciple. 'I do not know,' said the Master. 'Why should he be deemed a man of ideal virtue?' 2. 'When Ts'ui Tzŭ[8] put to death the Prince of Ch'i, although Ch'ên Wên Tzŭ held a fief of ten chariots he abandoned all and left the country. On reaching another state he said: "They are like our Minister Ts'ui Tzŭ," and left it. On reaching another state, he again said: "They are like our Minister Ts'ui Tzŭ," and left it. What would you say of him?' 'He was clean-handed,' said the Master. 'Was he a man of ideal virtue?' asked the disciple. 'I do not know,' answered the Master. 'Why should he be deemed a man of ideal virtue?'

---

[5] A contemporary of Confucius and minister of state.

[6] A minister of state, more superstitious.

[7] Tzŭ Wên was Prime Minister of Ch'u. Tradition says he was born a bastard, exposed, suckled by a tiger, and found by a prince, who brought him up. He never showed his emotions, but concerned himself entirely with his country's welfare, hence was perfect in loyalty. But that is not enough, says Confucius.

[8] Ch'ên Wên Tzŭ, minister of Ch'i, renounced all rather than live in rebellious states. Ts'ui Tzŭ, minister of Ch'i, murdered his prince, 548 B.C.

Chapter XIX

Chi Wên Tzŭ[9] used to think thrice before acting. The Master hearing of it said: 'Twice would do.'

Chapter XX

The Master said: 'While good order prevailed in his state, Ning Wu Tzŭ[10] was a wise man. When the state fell into disorder, he was a fool. His wisdom may be equalled, his folly cannot be equalled.'

Chapter XXI

When the Master was in the state of Ch'ên he said: 'Let us return! Let us return! My young people at home are ambitious and hasty; their culture acquires elegance, but they do not know how to shape affairs.'[11]

Chapter XXII

The Master said: 'Po I and Shu Ch'i[12] never bore ills in mind; hence those who bore them resentment were few.'

Chapter XXIII

The Master said: 'Who says that Wei-shang Kao[13] is upright? Some one begged vinegar of him, whereupon he begged it of a neighbour and gave that!'

Chapter XXIV

The Master said: 'Plausible speech, an ingratiating demeanour, and fulsome respect, — Tso Ch'iu Ming was ashamed of them; I, Ch'iu, also

---

[9] A minister in Lu.

[10] A minister in Wei.

[11] Confucius was in exile, about the age of 60, and had hopes of being recalled; instead of which the disciple Jan Ch'iu was bidden.

[12] Po I and Shu Ch'i were two princes of a small state at the end of the Shang dynasty. The throne was left to Shu Ch'i, who refused to take his elder brother's place. Po I likewise declined, and both withdrew from court. When King Wu the Good took up arms against the dissolute Chou Emperor, they still declined to join him, and died of starvation rather than dwell in a disloyal state. Admired by Confucius.

[13] A supposedly upright man, who nevertheless gave the condiment as if it were his own.

am ashamed of them.[14] To conceal one's resentment and yet appear friendly with a man, — Tso Ch'iu Ming was ashamed of it; I, Ch'iu, also am ashamed of it.'

CHAPTER XXV

1. Once when Yen Yüan and Tzŭ Lu were standing by him the Master said: 'Suppose each of you tells his wishes?' 2. 'I should like,' said Tzŭ Lu, 'to have carriages and horses and light furs to wear, so as to share them with my friends, nor would I feel any annoyance if they spoilt them.' 3. 'I should like,' said Yen Yüan, 'never to make a display of my good qualities, nor a parade of my merits.' 4. 'May we hear the Master's wishes?' asked Tzŭ Lu. 'They would be,' said the Master, 'to comfort the aged, be faithful to my friends, and cherish the young.'

CHAPTER XXVI

The Master said: 'It is all in vain! I have never yet seen a man who could perceive his own faults and bring the charge home against himself.'

CHAPTER XXVII

The Master said: 'Even in a hamlet of ten houses there must be men as conscientious and sincere as myself, but none as fond of learning as I am.'

[14] Tso Ch'iu Ming, an older disciple of Confucius. Ch'iu is Confucius himself, the name given by his mother, meaning 'Prominence', referring to the shape of his forehead.

BOOK VI

Concerning Certain Disciples and Other Subjects

CHAPTER I

1. The Master said: 'Yung! He is fit to occupy a ruler's seat.' 2. Chung Kung thereupon asked concerning Tzŭ-sang Po-tzŭ. 'He will do,' said the Master, 'but he is easy-going.' 3. 'For a man who is strict in his own life,' observed Chung Kung, 'to be easy in conduct in the surveillance of the people may, I suppose, be allowed? But he who is easy-going in private and easy-going in public, — that surely is sheer laxity?' 'Yung's statement is correct,' said the Master.[1]

CHAPTER II

Duke Ai[2] asked which of the disciples was fond of learning. Confucius answered him: 'There was Yen Hui, — he was fond of learning; he never visited his anger on another, and he never repeated a fault. Unfortunately his life was short and he died. Now there is none like him, nor have I heard of one who is fond of learning.'

CHAPTER III

1. Tzŭ Hua having been sent on a mission to the Ch'i State, Jan Tzŭ asked for grain for his mother. The Master said, 'Give her a *fu*.' He asked for more. 'Give her a *yü* then,' was the reply. Jan Tzŭ gave her five *ping*. 2. The Master remarked: 'On Ch'ih setting out for Ch'i he drove sleek horses and wore light furs. I have heard that the wise man succours the needy; he does not add to the rich.'

3. When Yüan Ssŭ was made governor of a certain place, the Master allowed him nine hundred measures of grain, which he declined. 4. 'Do

[1] Yung = Nan-Kung Kua: Chung Kung = Jan Yung: disciples. Of Tzŭ-sang Po-tzŭ nothing is known beyond this reference.

[2] Duke Ai, see I. xix.

not decline it,' said the Master. 'Can you not bestow it in your courts and hamlets, parishes, and villages?'[3]

Chapter IV

The Master speaking of Chung Kung[4] said: 'If the offspring of a brindled ox be ruddy and clean-horned, although men may not wish to use it, would the gods of the hills and streams reject it?'

Chapter V

The Master said, 'Hui! His heart for three months together never departed from virtue. As to the others, on some day or in some month they reached it, but that was all.'

Chapter VI

Chi K'ang Tzŭ asked whether Chung Yu were suited for employment in the administration. 'Yu is a man of decision,' said the Master. 'What difficulty would he find in the administration?' 'And T'zŭ?' he said, 'Is he suitable for the administration?' 'T'zŭ is a man of penetration,' was the answer. 'What difficulty would he find therein?' 'And Ch'iu?' he asked, 'Is he suitable for the administration?' 'Ch'iu is a man of much proficiency,' was the answer. 'What difficulty would he find therein?'[5]

Chapter VII

The head of the Chi clan sent to ask Min Tzŭ Ch'ien to be governor of Pi. Min Tzŭ Ch'ien replied, 'Courteously decline the offer for me. If any one comes for me again, then I shall certainly be far away: on the banks of the Wên River!'[6]

---

[3] Tzŭ Hua = Ch'ih. Jan Tzŭ or Jan Ch'iu was the clever but rather unscrupulous disciple. Yüan Ssŭ was the modest poor one of pure life.

[4] Chung Kung's father was notoriously mean; but his son was different and accepted by Confucius.

[5] Chi K'ang Tzŭ, the minister of Lu under Duke Ai, see II. xx, asks the characters of three disciples: Chung Yu, or Yu = Tzŭ Lu; Tzŭ = Tuan-mu Tzŭ, or Tzŭ Kung; Ch'iu = Jan Ch'iu. Tzŭ Lu and Jan Ch'iu became his officials, and did not always satisfy Confucius's ideals, specially Jan Ch'iu; e.g. see VI. x.: XVI. i.

[6] The head of the Chi clan was a usurper, while Min Tzŭ Ch'ien was noted for his purity of purpose.

Chapter VIII

When Po Niu was ill the Master went to inquire about him. Having grasped his hand through the window he said: 'We are losing him. Alas! It is the will of Heaven. That such a man should have such a disease! That such a man should have such a disease!'

Chapter IX

The Master said: 'What a man of worth was Hui![7] A single bamboo bowl of millet; a single ladle of cabbage soup; living in a mean alley! Others could not have borne his distress, but Hui never abated his cheerfulness. What a worthy man was Hui!'

Chapter X

Jan Ch'iu[8] remarked: 'It is not that I have no pleasure in your teaching, Sir, but I am not strong enough.' 'He who is not strong enough,' answered the Master, 'gives up half way, but you are drawing the line already.'

Chapter XI

The Master speaking to Tzŭ Hsia[9] said: 'Be you a scholar of the nobler type, not a scholar of the inferior man's type.'

Chapter XII

When Tzŭ Yu was governor of the city of Wu, the Master asked him: 'Have you been able to obtain men?' 'There is one Tan-t'ai Mieh-ming,' was the reply, 'who when walking takes no short cuts, and who, except on public business, has never yet come to my abode.'

Chapter XIII

The Master said: 'Mêng Chih-fan[10] is no boaster. When they were fleeing he brought up the rear, and only when about to enter the gate did he whip up his horse, saying: "It is not that I dare to be in the rear; my horse would not come on." '

---

[7] The favourite disciple, poor but a scholar, = Yen Yüan.

[8] See vi.

[9] An exact scholar, widely read, but precise rather than great.

[10] A brave minister of Lu who also went into exile at the same time as Confucius, and made this jest.

CHAPTER XIV

The Master said: 'Without the eloquence of T'o, the temple reader, and the beauty of Prince Chao[11] of Sung, it is hard to make headway in the present generation.'

CHAPTER XV

The Master said: 'Who can go forth except by the Door? Why will not men go by the Way?'

CHAPTER XVI

The Master said: 'When nature exceeds training, you have the rustic. When training exceeds nature, you have the clerk. It is only when nature and training are proportionately blended that you have the higher type of man.'

CHAPTER XVII

The Master said: 'Man is born for uprightness. Without it he is lucky to escape with his life!'

CHAPTER XVIII

The Master said: 'He who knows the truth is not equal to him who loves it, and he who loves it is not equal to him who delights in it.'

CHAPTER XIX

The Master said: 'To men above the average one may discourse on higher things; but to those who are below the average one may not discourse on higher things.'

CHAPTER XX

When Fan Ch'ih asked what constituted wisdom the Master replied: 'To devote oneself earnestly to one's duty to humanity and, while respecting the spirits of the departed, to avoid them, may be called wisdom.' On his asking about virtue, the Master replied: 'The man of virtue puts duty

[11] Prince Chao, a handsome decadent.

first, however difficult, and makes what he will gain thereby an after consideration — and this may be called virtue.'

Chapter XXI

The Master said: 'The clever delight in water, the virtuous in the hills; the clever are restless, the virtuous calm; the clever enjoy life, the virtuous prolong life.'

Chapter XXII

The Master said: 'The state of Ch'i, at one reform, could attain to the standard of Lu; but Lu, at one reform, could attain to ideal government.'

Chapter XXIII

The Master exclaimed: 'A wassail-bowl that is no longer used as a bowl! What a bowl! What a bowl!'[12]

Chapter XXIV

Tsai Wo[13] asked, saying: 'An altruist, even if some one said to him, "There is a man in the well," would, I suppose, go in after him?' 'Why should he act like that?' answered the Master. 'The higher type of man might hasten to the well, but not precipitate himself into it; he might be imposed upon, but not utterly hoodwinked.'

Chapter XXV

The Master said: 'The scholar who becomes widely versed in letters and who restrains his learning within the bounds of good conduct is not likely to leave the track.'

Chapter XXVI

When the Master went to see Nan-tzŭ,[14] Tzŭ Lu showed his displeasure, on which the Sage swore to him saying: 'If I have in any way done wrong, may Heaven reject me! May Heaven reject me!'

---

[12] Confucius refers to himself as a wassail-bowl that could well be used; but a bowl that is unused is a sad object.

[13] Tsai Wo, the lazy sceptical disciple.

[14] Nan-tzŭ, the beautiful dissolute wife of Duke Ling of Wei, whom Confucius as an official felt himself obliged to visit, as was the custom; to honest Tzŭ Lu's displeasure.

Chapter XXVII

The Master said: 'How perfect is the virtue that accords with the Golden Mean! And long has it been rare among the people!'

Chapter XXVIII

Tzŭ Kung said: 'Suppose there were one who conferred benefits far and wide upon the people, and who was able to succour the multitude, what might one say of him? Could he be called a philanthropist?' 'What has he to do with philanthropy?' said the Master. 'Must he not be a sage? Even Yao and Shun[15] felt their deficiency herein. 2. For the philanthropist is one who desiring to maintain himself sustains others, and desiring to develop himself develops others. 3. To be able from one's own self to draw a parallel for the treatment of others, — that may be called the rule of philanthropy.'

[15] Yao and Shun, the two great first rulers.

VOLUME IV

BOOK VII

Concerning the Master Himself

CHAPTER I

The Master said: 'As a transmitter, not an originator, a believer in and lover of antiquity, I venture to compare myself with our ancient worthy P'eng.'[1]

CHAPTER II

The Master said: 'The meditative treasuring up of knowledge, the unwearying pursuit of wisdom, the tireless instruction of others, — which of these is found in me?'

CHAPTER III

The Master said: 'Neglect in the cultivation of character, lack of thoroughness in study, incompetency to move towards recognized duty, inability to correct my imperfections, — these are what cause me solicitude.'

CHAPTER IV

In his leisure hours the Master relaxed his manner and wore a cheerful countenance.

CHAPTER V

The Master said: 'How utterly fallen off I am! For long I have not dreamed as of yore that I saw the Duke of Chou.'[2]

---

[1] P'eng was merely a high officer of the Shang dynasty who, tradition says, lived till he was 700 years old. Confucius, in his modesty, does not claim even to be equal with a great Sage of the past.

[2] Duke Wên of Chou was Confucius's ideal of a ruler. He established the Chou dynasty when Regent for his infant nephew, later King Wu. Sometimes called King Wên.

CHAPTER VI

1. The Master said: 'Fix your mind on the right way; 2. hold fast to it in your moral character; 3. follow it up in kindness to others; 4. take your recreation in the polite arts.'

CHAPTER VII

The Master said: 'From him who has brought his simple present of dried flesh seeking to enter my school, I have never withheld instruction.'

CHAPTER VIII

The Master said: 'I expound nothing to him who is not earnest, nor help out any one not anxious to express himself. When I have demonstrated one angle and he cannot bring me back the other three, then I do not repeat my lesson.'

CHAPTER IX

1. When the Master dined by the side of a mourner he never ate to the full. 2. On the same day that he had been mourning he never sang.

CHAPTER X

1. The Master addressing Yen Yüan said: 'To accept office when required, and to dwell in retirement when set aside, — only you and I have this spirit.' 2. 'But suppose,' said Tzŭ Lu, 'that the Master had the conduct of the armies of a great state, whom would he associate with him?' 3. 'The man,' replied the Master, 'who bare-armed would beard a tiger, or rush a river, dying without regret, — him I would not have with me. If I must have a colleague, he should be one who on the verge of an encounter would be apprehensive, and who loved strategy and its successful issue.'

CHAPTER XI

The Master said: 'If wealth were a thing one could count on finding, even though it meant my becoming a whip-holding groom, I would do it. As one cannot count on finding it, I will follow the quests that I love better.'

CHAPTER XII

The subjects which the Master treated with great solicitude were; — fasting, war, and disease.

CHAPTER XIII

When the Master was in Ch'i he heard the Shao music and for three months was unconscious of the taste of meat.[3] 'I did not imagine,' said he, 'that music had reached such perfection as this.'

CHAPTER XIV

1. Jan Yu asked: 'Is our Master for the Prince of Wei?'[4] 'Ah!' said Tzŭ Kung, 'I will just ask him.' 2. On entering he said: 'What sort of men were Po I and Shuh Ch'i?'[5] 'Worthies of old,' was the reply. 'Did they repine?' he asked. 'They sought virtue and they attained to virtue,' answered the Master; 'why then should they repine?' Tzŭ Kung went out and said: 'The Master is not for the Prince.'

CHAPTER XV

The Master said: 'With coarse food to eat, water for drink, and a bent arm for a pillow, — even in such a state I could be happy, for wealth and honour obtained unworthily are to me as a fleeting cloud.'

CHAPTER XVI

The Master said: 'Given a few more years of life to finish my study of the *Book of Changes*,[6] and I may be free from great errors.'

CHAPTER XVII

The subjects on which the Master most frequently discoursed were, — the Odes, the History, and the observances of the Rites; — on all these he constantly dwelt.

---

[3] Shao music, see III. xxv.

[4] Duke Ling of Wei's son tried to kill his notorious step-mother, Nan-tzŭ (see VI. xxvi, Note), and fled. Duke Ling died, and the state supported the grandson as ruler. His father thereupon returned and fought his own son for the throne, and won. Confucius was in Wei during this crisis, but regarded both son and grandson as unfilial and supported neither.

[5] Po I and Shu Ch'i, see V. xxii.

[6] The Book of Changes, or *I Ching*; astrological metaphysics.

Chapter XVIII

1. The Duke of Shê[7] asked Tzŭ Lu what he thought about Confucius, but Tzŭ Lu returned him no answer. 2. 'Why did you not say,' said the Master, 'he is simply a man so eager for improvement that he forgets his food, so happy therein that he forgets his sorrows, and so does not observe that old age is at hand?'

Chapter XIX

The Master said: 'I am not one who has innate knowledge, but one who, loving antiquity, is diligent in seeking it therein.'

Chapter XX

The Master would not discuss prodigies, prowess, lawlessness, or the supernatural.

Chapter XXI

The Master said: 'When walking in a party of three, my teachers are always present. I can select the good qualities of the one and copy them, and the unsatisfactory qualities of the other and correct them in myself.'

Chapter XXII

The Master said: 'Heaven begat the virtue that is in me. Huan T'ui,[8] — what can he do to me?'

Chapter XXIII

The Master said: 'My disciples! Do you think I possess something occult? I hide nothing occult from you. I do nothing that is not made known to you my disciples: — you have the real Ch'iu.[9]

Chapter XXIV

The Master took four subjects for his teaching, — culture, conduct, conscientiousness, and good faith.

---

[7] Shê was a very small state, and its ruler had arrogated to himself the title of duke.

[8] Huan T'ui, a minister of war, who, hating Confucius, had sent his men to pull a tree down upon Confucius by the roadside, during the exile: his brother, Ssŭ-ma Kêng, being a disciple.

[9] The real Ch'iu means Confucius himself.

CHAPTER XXV

The Master said: 'It is not mine to see an inspired man. Could I behold a noble man, I would be content.' 2. The Master said: 'It is not mine to see a really good man. Could I see a man of constant purpose, I would be content. 3. Affecting to have when they have not, empty yet affecting to be full, in straits yet affecting to be prosperous, — how hard it is for such men to have constancy of purpose!'

CHAPTER XXVI

The Master fished with a line, but not with a net; when shooting he did not aim at a resting bird.

CHAPTER XXVII

The Master said: 'There are men, probably, who do things correctly without knowing the reason why, but I am not like that: I hear much, select the good and follow it; I see much and treasure it up. This is the next best thing to philosophical knowledge.'

CHAPTER XXVIII

1. The people of Hu-hsiang were ill-conditioned folk; hence when a youth from there had an interview with the sage, the disciples wondered. 2. 'In sanctioning a man's entry here,' said the Master, 'I sanction nothing he may do on his withdrawal. Why, indeed, be so extreme? When a man cleanses himself and comes to me I may accept his present cleanness without becoming sponsor for his past.'

CHAPTER XXIX

The Master said: 'Is virtue indeed afar off? I crave for virtue and lo! virtue is at hand.'

CHAPTER XXX

1. The minister of justice of the state of Ch'ên asked whether Duke Chao knew the Regulations. 'He knew them,' replied Confucius. 2. When Confucius had withdrawn, the Minister bowed to Wu-ma Ch'i to come forward and said: 'I have heard that a man of noble parts is not biased. May then a noble man be yet biased? Duke Chao took his wife

from the house of Wu, of the same surname as himself, and spoke of her as the elder Lady Tzŭ of Wu. If the duke knew the Regulations, who does not know them?' 3. Wu-ma Ch'i reported this, whereupon the Master remarked: 'I am fortunate. If I make a mistake, people are sure to know of it!'[10]

Chapter XXXI

When the Master was in company with any one who was singing and the piece was good, he always had it repeated, joining in the melody himself.

Chapter XXXII

The Master said: 'In literature perhaps I may compare with others, but as to my living the noble life, to that I have not yet attained.'

Chapter XXXIII

The Master said: 'As to being a sage, or a man of virtue, how dare I presume to such a claim? But as to striving thereafter unwearyingly, and teaching others therein without flagging, — that can be said of me, and that is all.' 'And that,' said Kung-hsi Hua, 'is just what we disciples cannot learn.'

Chapter XXXIV

Once when the Master was seriously ill Tzŭ Lu asked leave to have prayers offered. 'Is there authority for such a step?' asked the Master. 'There is,' Tzŭ Lu replied. 'In the litanies it is said, "We pray to you, spirits celestial and terrestrial".' The Master answered, 'My praying has been for long.'

Chapter XXXV

The Master said: 'Men, if prodigal, are uncontrolled; if frugal then narrow: but better be narrow than uncontrolled.'

---

10 This must have occurred in 493 B.C., during Confucius's stay in Ch'ên. For Duke Chao of Lu Confucius had gone into his first exile sixteen years before: how could he do aught but parry criticism of him? By Chinese regulations marriage is forbidden between people of the same personal name. Duke Chao of the House of Wu avoided this by calling his bride Lady Tzŭ of Wu. This was a ruse, and all knew it.

Chapter XXXVI

The Master said: 'The noble man is calm and serene, the inferior man is continually worried and anxious.'

Chapter XXXVII

The Master was affable yet dignified, commanding yet not overbearing, courteous yet easy.

BOOK VIII

Chiefly Concerning Certain Ancient Worthies

Chapter I

The Master said: 'T'ai Po[1] may be described as possessing a character of the noblest. He resolutely renounced the imperial throne, leaving people no ground for appreciating his conduct.'

Chapter II

1. The Master said: 'Courtesy uncontrolled by the laws of good taste becomes laboured effort, caution uncontrolled becomes timidity, boldness uncontrolled becomes recklessness, and frankness uncontrolled becomes effrontery. 2. When the highly placed pay generous regard to their own families, the people are equally stirred to kindness. When they do not discard old dependants, neither will the people deal meanly with theirs.'

Chapter III

When the philosopher Tsêng was taken ill, he called his disciples and said: 'Uncover my feet, uncover my arms. The Ode says:

> "Be anxious, be cautious,
> As when near a deep gulf,
> As when treading thin ice."

But from henceforth I know I shall escape all injury, my disciples.'[2]

---

[1] T'ai Po renounced the succession in ancient days because his views on loyalty to the Shang emperors differed from his father's; yet he gave no reason in public.

[2] The disciple Tsêng Tzŭ thought of his body as a gift from his parents, to be kept unharmed and intact. He shows his disciples his limbs entire. Chinese still follow this idea.

Chapter IV

1. During Tsêng Tzŭ's illness Mêng Ching Tzŭ[3] called to make inquiries. 2. Tsêng Tzŭ spoke to him saying: 'When a bird is dying, its song is sad. When a man is dying, what he says is worth listening to. 3. The three rules of conduct upon which a man of high rank should place value are, — in his bearing to avoid rudeness and remissness, in ordering his looks to aim at sincerity, and in the tone of his conversation to keep aloof from vulgarity and impropriety. As to the details of temple vessels, — there are proper officers for looking after them.'

Chapter V

Tsêng Tzŭ said: 'Talented, yet seeking knowledge from the untalented; of many attainments, yet seeking knowledge from those with few; having, as though he had not; full, yet bearing himself as if empty; offended against, yet not retaliating, — once upon a time I had a friend who lived after this manner.'

Chapter VI

Tsêng Tzŭ said: 'The man to whom one could entrust a young orphan prince and delegate the command over a hundred *li*, yet whom the advent of no emergency, however great, could shake, — would he be a man of the nobler order? Of the nobler order he would certainly be.'

Chapter VII

1. Tsêng Tzŭ said: 'The scholar must not be without capacity and fortitude, for his load is heavy and the road is long. 2. He takes virtue for his load, and is not that heavy? Only with death does his course end, and is not that long?'

Chapter VIII

1. The Master said: 'Let the character be formed by the poets; 2. established by the laws of right behaviour; 3. and perfected by music.'

Chapter IX

The Master said: 'The people may be made to follow a course, but not to understand the reason why.'

---

[3] Mêng Ching Tzŭ, a young minister of Lu, and son of Mêng Wu Po, see II. vi.

Chapter X

The Master said: 'Love of daring and resentment of poverty drive men to desperate deeds; and men who lack moral character, if resentment of them be carried too far, will be driven to similar deeds.'

Chapter XI

The Master said: 'If a man have gifts as admirable as those of Duke Chou,[4] yet be vain and mean, his other gifts are unworthy of notice.'

Chapter XII

The Master said: 'It is not easy to find a man who has studied for three years without aiming at pay.'

Chapter XIII

1. The Master said: 'The man of unwavering sincerity and love of moral discipline will keep to the death his excellent principles. 2. He will not enter a tottering state nor dwell in a rebellious one. When law and order prevail in the empire, he is in evidence. When it is without law and order, he withdraws. 3. When law and order prevail in his state, he is ashamed to be needy and of no account. When law and order fail, he is ashamed to be in affluence and honour.'

Chapter XIV

The Master said: 'He who does not occupy the office does not discuss its policy.'

Chapter XV

The Master said: 'When the bandmaster Chih entered on his duties, how the closing strains of the Kuan Chü filled the ear with the grandeur of their volume!'[5]

[4] Duke Chou = Duke Wên of Chou, see VII. v.

[5] Remark made probably after Confucius's return and reorganization of the music in Lu.

Chapter XVI

The Master said: 'With the impulsive yet evasive, the simple yet dishonest, the stupid yet untruthful, I hold no acquaintance.'

Chapter XVII

The Master said: 'Learn as if you were not reaching your goal, and as though you were afraid of missing it.'

Chapter XVIII

The Master said: 'How sublime the way Shun and Yü undertook the empire, and yet as if it were nothing to them!'[6]

Chapter XIX

1. The Master said: 'Great indeed was the sovereignty of Yao! How sublime he was! Only Heaven is great, and only Yao answers to its standard. How vast he was! Beyond the power of the people to express! 2. How sublime were his achievements! How brilliant his civilizing regulations!'

Chapter XX

1. Shun had five ministers and the empire was well ruled. 2. King Wu remarked: 'I have ten adjutants, able administrators.' 3. Confucius said: 'Is it not a true saying that talent is hard to find? Yet only at the transition of the T'ang Dynasty into the Yü was it richer in talent than at the founding of the Chou, when indeed one of its ministers was a woman, so that in reality there were only nine men. 4. Possessor of two of the empire's three parts, with which he submissively served the dynasty of Yin, the virtue of the founder of the Chou may indeed be called perfect virtue.'

---

[6] xviii-xxi. Shun and Yü were great servants of the state in semi-mythical times. Both controlled the floods, ordained laws, and divided the land into provinces. Yao, Emperor, 2356 B.C., first unified the state and set forth the Calendar of 366 days. King Wu founded the Chou dynasty 1122 B.C., but had long delayed rebelling against the last debauched Yin Emperor. The Emperor Yü was noted for simplicity of life.

Chapter XXI

The Master said: 'In Yü I can find no room for criticism. Simple in his own food and drink, he was unsparing in his filial offerings to the spirits. Shabby in his workaday clothes he was most scrupulous as to the elegance of his kneeling-apron and sacrificial crown. Humble as to the character of his palace, he spent his strength in the draining and ditching of the country. In Yü I find no room for criticism.'

VOLUME V

BOOK IX

Chiefly Personal

Chapter I

The Master seldom spoke on profit, on the orderings of Providence, and on perfection.

Chapter II

1. A man of the village of Ta-hsiang remarked: 'What a great man is K'ung, the Philosopher. Yet though his learning is vast, in nothing does he acquire a reputation.' 2. The Master on hearing it, addressing his disciples, said: 'What shall I take up? Shall I take to driving? Or shall I take to archery? I will take to driving.'

Chapter III

1. The Master said: 'A linen cap is the prescribed form, but nowadays silk is worn. This saves expense, and I follow the general usage. 2. Salutation below the audience hall is the prescribed form, but now they salute above. This is assumption, and therefore, though infringing the general usage, I follow the rule of bowing below.'

Chapter IV

The Master was entirely free from four things: he had no preconceptions, no predeterminations, no obduracy, and no egoism.

Chapter V

1. When the Master was in jeopardy in K'uang, 2. he said, 'Since King Wên is no longer alive, does not the mantle of enlightenment (*wên*) rest here on me? 3. If heaven were going to destroy this enlightenment, a

mortal like me would not have obtained such a connexion with it. Since heaven is not ready to destroy this enlightenment, what can the men of K'uang do to me?'[1]

CHAPTER VI

1. A great minister inquired of Tzŭ Kung saying, 'Your Master, — he is surely inspired? What varied acquirements he has!' 2. Tzŭ Kung answered, 'Of a truth Heaven has lavishly endowed him, to the point of inspiration, and his acquirements are also many.' 3. When the Master heard of it, he said: 'Does the minister really know me? In my youth I was in humble circumstances, and for that reason gained a variety of acquirements, — in common matters: but does nobleness of character depend on variety? It does not depend on variety.' 4. Lao[2] said, 'The Master used to say, "I have not been occupied in official life, and so have had time to become acquainted with the arts!" '

CHAPTER VII

The Master said: 'Am I indeed a man with innate knowledge? I have no such knowledge; but when an uncultivated person, in all simplicity, comes to me with a question, I thrash out its pros and cons until I fathom it.'

CHAPTER VIII

The Master said: 'The phoenix comes not, the river manifests no directing plan. All is over with my hopes!'[3]

CHAPTER IX

Whenever he saw a person in mourning, or in official cap and robes, or one who was blind, the Master on noticing him, even though the man were his own junior, always arose; or, if he were passing such a one, he always quickened his steps.

---

[1] During the exile, the Master came to K'uang, where a mistaken facial resemblance to an oppressor, Yang Huo, caused the inhabitants to put him and the disciples into danger. For King Wên, see VII. v, Note.

[2] The only mention of the disciple Lao, or Ch'in Chang.

[3] No supernatural sign is given for him.

Chapter XXI

The Master said: 'There are blades that spring up and never flower, and there are others that flower but never fruit.'

Chapter XXII

The Master said: 'The young should inspire one with respect. How do we know that their future will not equal our present? But if a man has reached forty or fifty without being heard of, he, indeed, is incapable of commanding respect!'

Chapter XXIII

The Master said: 'Can any one refuse assent to words of just admonition? But it is amendment that is of value. Can any one be otherwise than pleased with advice persuasively offered? But it is the application that is of value. Mere interest without application, mere assent without amendment,—I can do nothing whatever with men of such calibre.'

Chapter XXIV

The Master said: 'Make conscientiousness and sincerity your leading principles. Have no friends inferior to yourself. And when in the wrong, do not hesitate to amend.'

Chapter XXV

The Master said: 'You may rob a three corps army of its commander-in-chief, but you cannot rob even a common man of his will.'

Chapter XXVI

1. The Master said: 'Wearing a shabby, hemp-quilted robe, and standing by others dressed in fox and badger, yet in no way abashed,—Yu[9] would be the one for that, eh? 2. Unfriendly to none, and courting none, what does he that is not excellent?' 3. As Tzŭ Lu afterwards was perpetually intoning this, the Master observed: 'But how can those two points alone be sufficient for excellence?'

---

[9] Tzŭ Lu = Yu.

CHAPTER XXVII

The Master said: 'Only when the year grows cold do we realize that the pine and the cypress are the last to fade.'

CHAPTER XXVIII

The Master said: 'The enlightened are free from doubt, the virtuous from anxiety, and the brave from fear.'

CHAPTER XXIX

The Master said: 'There are some with whom one can associate in study, but who are not yet able to make common advance towards the truth: there are others who can make common advance towards the truth, but who are not yet able to take with you a like firm stand; and there are others with whom you can take such a firm stand, but with whom you cannot associate in judgement.'

CHAPTER XXX

1. 'The blossoms on the cherry tree
Are changing and quivering,
Can I do aught but think of thee
In thy far-distant dwelling?'[10]

2. The Master said: 'The poet had never really bestowed a thought. If he had, what distance would have existed?'

[10] From one of the poems not included in the classical Canon.

BOOK X

Concerning the Sage in His Daily Life

Chapter I

1. Confucius in his native village bore himself with simplicity, as if he had no gifts of speech. 2. But when in the temple or at court, he expressed himself readily and clearly, yet with a measure of reserve.

Chapter II

1. At court, when conversing with ministers of his own rank, he spoke out boldly; when conversing with the higher ministers he spoke respectfully; 2. but when the prince was present, his movements were nervous, though self-possessed.

Chapter III

1. When the prince summoned him to receive a visitor, his expression seemed to change, and his knees as it were bent under him. 2. As he saluted those who stood with him, on the right hand or the left as occasion required, his robe in front and behind hung straight and undisturbed; 3. and, as he hastened forward, it was as if with outstretched wings. 4. When the visitor had departed he always reported, saying, 'The Guest is no longer looking back at us.'

Chapter IV

1. On entering the palace gate he appeared to stoop, as though the gate were not high enough to admit him. 2. He never stood in the middle of the gateway, nor in going through did he step on the sill. 3. As he passed the throne he wore a constrained expression, his knees appeared to bend, and words seemed to fail him. 4. As he ascended the audience hall, holding up his skirt, he appeared to stoop, and he held his breath as if he dare not breathe. 5. On coming forth from his audience, after descending the first step, his expression relaxed into

one of relief; at the bottom of the steps he hastened forward as with outstretched wings, and on regaining his place he maintained an attitude of nervous respect.

Chapter V

1. He carried the ducal mace with bent back, as if unequal to its weight, neither higher than when making a bow, nor lower than when offering a gift: his expression, too, was perturbed and anxious, and he dragged his feet as if something were trailing behind. 2. While offering the presents with which he was commissioned he wore an easy look; 3. and at the subsequent private audience he bore himself with amiability.

Chapter VI

1. He did not wear facings of purple or mauve, 2. nor even in undress did he use red or crimson. 3. In the hot weather he wore an unlined gown of fine or loose-woven material, but always outside and over another. 4. With a black robe he wore black lambskin, with a light robe fawn, and with a yellow robe fox. 5. His undress fur gown was long, with the right sleeve cut short. 6. He always had his sleeping-garment made half as long again as his body. 7. He had thick fox or badger for home wear. 8. When out of mourning he omitted none of the usual ornaments. 9. His skirts, all save his court skirt, he always shaped towards the waist. 10. He did not pay visits of condolence in dark lamb's fur or a dark hat. 11. At the new moon he always put on his court robes and presented himself at court.

Chapter VII

1. When fasting he always wore a spotless suit of linen cloth. 2. When fasting, too, he always altered his diet, and in his dwelling always changed his seat.

Chapter VIII

1. He had no objection to his rice being of the finest, nor to having his meat finely minced. 2. Rice affected by the weather, or turned, he would not eat, nor fish that was unsound, nor flesh that was tainted. Neither would he eat anything discoloured, nor that smelt, nor that was under-

or over-cooked, or not in season. 3. He would not eat anything improperly cut, nor anything served without its proper seasoning. 4. However much meat there might be, he did not allow what he took to exceed the flavour of the rice; only in wine he had no set limit, short of mental confusion. 5. Bought wine or dried meat from the market he would not eat. 6. He was never without ginger at his meals; 7. but he was not a great eater. 8. After the sacrifices in the ducal temple he never kept his share of the flesh overnight, nor the flesh of his ancestral sacrifices more than three days, lest after three days it might not be eaten. 9. He did not converse while eating, nor talk when in bed. 10. Though his food were only coarse rice and vegetable broth, he invariably offered a little in sacrifice, and always with solemnity.

Chapter IX

He would not sit on his mat unless it were straight.

Chapter X

1. When his fellow villagers had a feast he only left after the elders had departed. 2. When his fellow villagers held a procession to expel the pestilential influences, he put on his court robes and stood on the eastern steps.

Chapter XI

1. When sending complimentary inquiries to any one in another state, he bowed twice as he escorted his messenger forth. 2. On K'ang Tzŭ sending him a present of medicine he bowed and accepted it, but said: 'As I am not well acquainted with it, I do not dare to taste it.'[1]

Chapter XII

When his stable was burnt down, on coming forth from the Audience he asked, 'Is any one hurt?' He did not ask about the horses.

[1] K'ang Tzŭ = Chi K'ang Tzŭ, the minister to Duke Ai of Lu. The polite custom was to acknowledge edible presents by at once tasting them.

CHAPTER XIII

1. When the prince sent him a present of food, he always adjusted his mat and first tasted it himself; but if the prince's present were fresh meat, he always had it cooked, and set it before his ancestors. Were the prince's present living, he always kept it alive. 2. When in attendance on the prince at a state dinner, while the prince sacrificed he acted the subordinate part of first tasting the dishes. 3. When he was ill and the prince came to see him, he had his head laid to the east, and his court robes thrown over him, with his sash drawn across. 4. When his prince commanded his presence, he did not wait while his carriage was being yoked, but started on foot.

CHAPTER XIV

On entering the imperial Ancestral Temple, he asked about every detail.

CHAPTER XV

1. When a friend died, with no one to see to the rites, he would say, 'I will see to his funeral.' 2. On receiving a present from a friend, unless it were sacrificial flesh, he never made obeisance, not even if it were a carriage and horses.

CHAPTER XVI

1. In bed he did not lie like a corpse. At home he wore no formal air. 2. Whenever he saw any one in mourning, even though it were an intimate acquaintance, his expression always changed, and when he saw any one in a cap of state, or a blind man, even though not in public, he always showed respect. 3. On meeting any one in deep mourning, he would bow to the crossbar of his carriage, as he did also to any one carrying the census boards. 4. When entertained at a rich repast, he always expressed his appreciation with an altered look and by standing up. 5. On a sudden clap of thunder, or a violent storm of wind, his countenance always changed.

CHAPTER XVII

1. When mounting his carriage he always stood correctly, holding the mounting-cord in his hand. 2. In the carriage he did not look behind, nor speak hastily, nor point with his hands.

Chapter XVIII

1. Seeing their faces it rose, hovered about and settled again. 2. The Master remarked: 'Ah! hen-pheasant on the hill bridge, you know your time! You know your time!' 3. Tzŭ Lu motioned towards it, whereupon it smelt at him three times and rose.[2]

[2] A passage of acknowledged difficulty; one suggestion being that Tzŭ Lu caught and cooked the hen pheasant, Confucius smelt it thrice, and rose—not eating.

VOLUME VI

BOOK XI

Chiefly Concerning the Disciples

CHAPTER I

1. The Master observed: 'In the arts of civilization our forerunners are esteemed uncultivated, while in those arts, their successors are looked upon as cultured gentlemen. 2. But when I have need of those arts, I follow our forerunners.'

CHAPTER II

1. The Master said: 'Of all who were with me in Ch'ên and Ch'ai, not one now comes to my door.' 2. Noted for moral character there were Yen Yüan, Min Tzŭ Ch'ien, Jan Niu and Chung Kung; for gifts of speech Tsai Wo and Tzŭ Kung; for administrative ability Jan Yu and Chi Lu; and for literature and learning Tzŭ Yu and Tzŭ Hsia.[1]

CHAPTER III

The Master said: 'Hui was not one who gave me any assistance. He was invariably satisfied with whatever I said.'

CHAPTER IV

The Master said: 'What a filial son Min Tzŭ Ch'ien has been! No one takes exception to what his parents and brothers have said of him!'

---

[1] A remark made in old age about the disciples who were with him in exile. A famous list of 'the ten discerning ones' amongst the disciples, except that Tsêng Tzŭ is not mentioned.

CHAPTER V

Nan Yung frequently repeated the White Sceptre Ode. Confucius gave him his elder brother's daughter to wife.[2]

CHAPTER VI

Once when Chi K'ang Tzŭ[3] asked which of the disciples was fond of learning, the Master replied: 'There was Yen Hui who was fond of learning, but unhappily his life was cut short and he died, — now there is none.'

CHAPTER VII

1. When Yen Yüan died, Yen Lu[4] begged for the Master's carriage in order to sell it and purchase an outer shell. 2. The Master answered: 'Gifted or not gifted, every one considers his own son. When my son Li died, he had a coffin but no shell. I did not walk on foot to provide a shell for him, for I have to follow behind the great officers of state and may not go afoot.'

CHAPTER VIII

When Yen Yüan died the Master said: 'Alas! Heaven has bereft me; Heaven has bereft me.'

CHAPTER IX

1. When Yen Yüan died the Master bewailed him with exceeding grief, whereupon his followers said to him, 'Sir! You are carrying your grief to excess.' 2. 'Have I gone to excess?' asked he. 3. 'But if I may not grieve exceedingly over this man, for whom shall I grieve?'

---

[2] The couplet that Nan Yung chanted thrice daily, ran:

'The White Sceptre's flaw may be ground away,
But a flaw in my words has no remedy.'

[3] Chi K'ang Tzŭ, the minister, see II. xx, Note.

[4] vii–x. Yen Lu, father of the beloved disciple, Yen Yüan, wanted a grand funeral for his son when he died. Confucius replied that he had not sold his carriage even for his own son's funeral the preceding year, as state position obliged him to keep it. But the disciples buried him with much pomp, with Confucius bewailing that they should thus do; for Yen Yüan (Hui) would have understood a simple cortège.

CHAPTER X

1. When Yen Hui died the other disciples proposed to give him an imposing funeral, to which the Master said: 'It will not do.' 2. Nevertheless they buried him with pomp. 3. 'Hui!' said the Master, 'You regarded me as a father, while I am not permitted to regard you as my son. But it is not I who do this. It is these disciples.'

CHAPTER XI

When Chi Lu[5] asked about his duty to the spirits the Master replied: 'While still unable to do your duty to the living, how can you do your duty to the dead?' When he ventured to ask about death, Confucius answered: 'Not yet understanding life, how can you understand death?'

CHAPTER XII

1. Once when Min Tzŭ was standing by the Master's side he looked so self-reliant, Tzŭ Lu so full of energy, and Jan Yu and Tzŭ Kung so frank and fearless that the Master was highly gratified. 2. 'But,' said he, 'a man like Yu[6] will not come to a natural death.'

CHAPTER XIII

1. When the men of Lu were for rebuilding the Long Treasury, 2. Min Tzŭ Ch'ien observed, 'How would it do to restore it as before? Why need it be reconstructed?' 3. The Master said: 'This man seldom speaks, but when he does he is sure to hit the mark.'

CHAPTER XIV

1. The Master said: 'What is Yu's[7] harp doing in my school?' 2. The other disciples on hearing this ceased to respect Tzŭ Lu, whereupon the Master said: 'Yu! he has ascended the hall, though he has not yet entered the inner rooms.'

[5] Chi Lu = Tzŭ Lu.
[6] Yu = Tzŭ Lu.
[7] Yu (Tzŭ Lu), the soldier, liked martial music.

Chapter XV

1. Tzŭ Kung asked which was the better, Shih or Shang?[8] The Master replied: 'Shih exceeds, Shang comes short.' 2. 'So then,' queried he, 'Shih surpasses Shang, eh?' 3. 'To go beyond the mark,' replied the Master, 'is as bad as to come short of it.'

Chapter XVI

1. The Chief of the Chi clan was richer than Duke Chou had been, yet the disciple Ch'iu[9] collected his revenues for him and kept on still further increasing his income. 2. 'He is no disciple of mine,' said the Master. 'You may beat the drum, my sons, and attack him.'

Chapter XVII

1. Ch'ai was simple-minded; 2. Shên dull; 3. Shih shallow; 4. Yu unrefined.[10]

Chapter XVIII

1. The Master said: 'Hui![11] he was almost perfect, yet he was often in want. 2. Tz'ŭ was not content with his lot, and yet his goods increased abundantly; nevertheless in his judgements he often hit the mark.'

Chapter XIX

When Tzŭ Chang asked what characterized the way of the man of natural goodness, the Master replied: 'He does not tread the beaten track, nor yet does he enter into the inner sanctum of philosophy.'

---

[8] Two learned disciples. Shih = Tzŭ Chang, well spoken of by Tzŭ Kung for his humility. Shang = Pu Shang, or Tzŭ Hsia, several sayings of whose occur in Book XIX.

[9] Ch'iu = Jan Ch'iu, the clever unscrupulous disciple. Duke Chou was rich by right of imperial state.

[10] The characters of four disciples when they entered the school of Confucius originally: Ch'ai = Kao Ch'ai, or Tzŭ Kao; Shên = the great disciple Tsêng Tzŭ, or Tsêng Shên; Shih = Tzŭ Chang, well spoken of later by Tzŭ Kung for his humility and diligence; Yu = Tzŭ Lu, the soldier who became philosopher.

[11] Hui = Yen Yüan. Tz'ŭ = Tzŭ Kung.

CHAPTER XX

The Master said: 'That a man's address may be solid and reliable, this one may grant; but does it follow that he is a man of the higher type, or is his seriousness only in appearance?'

CHAPTER XXI

When Tzŭ Lu asked whether he should put what he heard into immediate practice, the Master answered, 'You have parents and elders still living, why should you at once put all you hear into practice?' When Jan Yu asked whether he should put what he heard into immediate practice, the Master answered, 'Put what you hear at once into practice.' Kung-hsi Hua asked: 'When Yu asked if he should put the precepts he heard into immediate practice, you, Sir, replied, "You have parents and elders alive"; but when Ch'iu asked if he should put the precepts he heard into immediate practice, you, Sir, replied, "Put what you hear at once into practice." As I am perplexed about your meaning I venture to ask a solution.' 'Ch'iu,' answered the Master, 'lags behind, so I urged him forward; but Yu has energy for two men, so I held him back.'

CHAPTER XXII

When the Master was put in peril in K'uang, Yen Hui fell behind. On the Master saying to him, 'I thought you were dead,' he replied, 'While you, Sir, live, how should I dare to die?'

CHAPTER XXIII

1. When Chi Tzŭ-jan[12] asked if Chung Yu and Jan Ch'iu could be called great ministers, 2. the Master replied, 'I thought, Sir, you were going to ask about something extraordinary, and it is only a question about Yu and Ch'iu. 3. He who may be called a great minister is one who serves his prince according to the right, and when that cannot be, resigns. 4. Now, as for Yu and Ch'iu, they may be styled ordinary ministers.' 5. 'So, then,' said Tzŭ Jan, 'they would follow their chief, eh?' 6. 'A parricide or regicide,' answered the Master, 'they would assuredly not follow, however.'

---

[12] Chi Tzŭ-jan is the younger brother of Chi K'ang Tzŭ, the minister, see II. xx, Note. He asks about the characters of Tzŭ Lu (Chung Yu) and Jan Ch'iu: the family was meditating getting rid of their prince.

CHAPTER XXIV

1. When Tzŭ Lu obtained the appointment of Tzŭ Kao[13] as governor of Pi, 2. the Master said, 'You are doing an ill turn to another man's son.' 3. 'He will have his people and officers,' replied Tzŭ Lu, 'he will also have the altars of the land and the grain, why must he read books before he is considered educated?' 4. 'It is because of this kind of talk,' said the Master, 'that I hate glib people.'

CHAPTER XXV

1. Once when Tzŭ Lu, Tsêng Shih, Jan Yu, and Kung-hsi Hua were seated with the Master, 2. he said, 'You no doubt consider me a day or so your senior, but pray do not so consider me. 3. Living in private life you are each saying: "I am unknown." Now suppose some prince were to take notice of you, what would you like to do?' 4. Tzŭ Lu in off-hand manner replied, 'Give me a kingdom of a thousand chariots, hemmed in by two great powers, oppressed by invading troops, with famine superadded, and let me have its administration,—in three years' time I could make it brave and, moreover, make it know the right course to pursue.' The Master smiled at him. 5. 'And how about you, Ch'iu?' 'Give me a district of sixty or seventy *li* square,' answered he, 'or say, one of fifty or sixty *li* square, and let me have its administration,—in three years' time I could make its people dwell in plenty; but as to the arts of civilization, I should have to await a nobler man.' 6. 'And how about you, Ch'ih?' 'I do not say that I could do it,' answered he, 'but I should like to learn. I would like at the service in the great Ancestral Temple, or say, at the Prince's imperial audience, to take part, in cap and gown, as a minor assistant.' 7. 'And how about you, Tien?' Pausing as he thrummed his harp, its notes still vibrating, he left the instrument, arose, and replied, saying, 'My wishes are different from those presented by these three gentlemen.' 'What harm in that?' said the Master. 'Let each name his desire.' 'Mine would be,' he said, 'towards the end of Spring, with the dress of the season all complete, along with five or six newly capped young men, and six or seven youths, to bathe in the River I, enjoy the breezes among the Rain Altars, and return home singing.' The Master heaved a deep sigh and said, 'I am with Tien.' 8. When the three others withdrew, Tsêng Shih remained behind and asked, 'What do you think of the remarks of these three disciples?' The Master answered, 'Well, each of them merely stated his aspirations.' 9. 'Then why did you smile,

[13] Tzŭ Kao was the ugly dwarfish disciple.

Sir, at Yu?' he pursued. 10. 'The administration of a country demands a right bearing,' was the reply, 'but his speech lacked modesty,—that is why I smiled at him.' 11. 'But Ch'iu,—was it not a state that he wanted?' 'Where do you see a district of sixty or seventy, or of fifty or sixty *li* that is not a state?' was the answer. 12. 'And Ch'ih,—was it not a state that he wanted?' 'In the Ancestral Temple and at the prince's audience, who but a prince takes a part?' was the reply. 'Yet if Ch'ih were to act a minor part who could act the major?'[14]

[14] Again the characters of the disciples come out. Tzŭ Lu talks of military prowess. Jan Ch'iu wants to enrich an administration. Ch'ih, or Kung-hsi Hua, loved the services of the temple. Tien, or Tsêng Tien, father of the disciple Tsêng Tzŭ, longs for happy companionship and strolling in early summer.

BOOK XII

Concerning Virtue, Nobility, and Polity

CHAPTER I

1. When Yen Yüan asked the meaning of virtue, the Master replied: 'Virtue is the denial of self and response to what is right and proper. Deny yourself for one day and respond to the right and proper, and everybody will accord you virtuous. For has virtue its source in oneself, or is it forsooth derived from others?' 2. 'May I beg for the main features?' asked Yen Yüan. The Master answered: 'When wrong and improper do not look, when wrong and improper do not listen, when wrong and improper do not speak, when wrong and improper do not move.' 'Though I am not clever,' said Yen Yüan, 'permit me to carry out these precepts.'

CHAPTER II

When Chung Kung asked the meaning of virtue, the Master said: 'When abroad, behave as if interviewing an honoured guest; in directing the people, act as if officiating at a great sacrifice; do not do to others what you would not like yourself; then your public life will arouse no ill-will nor your private life any resentment.' 'Though I am not clever,' replied Chung Kung, 'permit me to carry out these precepts.'

CHAPTER III

1. When Ssŭ-ma Niu asked for a definition of virtue, 2. the Master said: 'The man of virtue is chary of speech.' 3. 'He is chary of speech! Is this the meaning of virtue?' demanded Niu. 'When the doing of it is difficult,' responded Confucius, 'can one be other than chary of talking about it?'

Chapter IV

1. When Ssŭ-ma Niu asked for a definition of the man of noble mind, the Master said: 'The man of noble mind has neither anxiety nor fear.' 2. 'Neither anxiety nor fear!' he rejoined. 'Is this the definition of a noble man?' 'On searching within,' replied the Master, 'he finds no chronic ill, so why should he be anxious or why should he be afraid?'

Chapter V

1. Once when Ssŭ-ma Niu sorrowfully remarked, 'Other men all have their brothers, I alone am without,' 2. Tzŭ Hsia responded: 'I have heard it said, 3. "Death and life are divine dispensations, and wealth and honours are with Heaven. 4. When the man of noble mind unfailingly conducts himself with self-respect, and is courteous and well-behaved with others, then all within the four seas are his brothers. How, then, can a fine man grieve that he is without a brother?" '[1]

Chapter VI

When Tzŭ Chang asked what was meant by insight, the Master replied: 'He who is unmoved by the insidious soaking in of slander, or by urgent representations of direct personal injury, may truly be called a man of insight. Indeed, he who is unmoved by the insidious soaking in of slander or by urgent representations of direct personal injury, may also indeed be called far-sighted.'

Chapter VII

1. When Tzŭ Kung asked what were the essentials of government, the Master replied: 'Sufficient food, sufficient forces, and the confidence of the people.'

2. 'Suppose,' rejoined Tzŭ Kung, 'I were compelled to dispense with one, which of these three should I forgo first?' 'Forgo the forces,' was the reply.

3. 'Suppose,' said Tzŭ Kung, 'I were compelled to eliminate another, which of the other two should I forgo?' 'The food,' was the reply; 'for from of old death has been the lot of all men, but a people without faith cannot stand.'

---

[1] Ssŭ-ma Niu's brother, Huan T'ui, had tried to kill Confucius. Tzŭ Hsia comforts him nobly.

Chapter VIII

1. Chi Tzŭ-Ch'êng[2] remarked: 'For a man of high character to be natural is quite sufficient; what need is there of art to make him such?'

2. 'Alas!' said Tzŭ Kung, 'Your Excellency's words are those of a noble man, but a team of four horses cannot overtake the tongue. 3. Art, as it were, is nature; as nature, so to speak, is art. The hairless hide of a tiger or a leopard is about the same as the hide of a dog or a sheep.'

Chapter IX

1. Duke Ai[3] inquired of Yu Jo[4] saying: 'It is a year of dearth, and we have not revenue enough for our needs; what is to be done?' 2. 'Why not simply tithe the land?' replied Yu Jo. 3. 'Why, with two-tenths,' said the Duke, 'I have still not enough, how could I manage with the one-tenth system?' 4. 'If the people enjoy plenty,' was the rejoinder, 'with whom will the prince share want? But if the people are in want, with whom will the prince share plenty?'

Chapter X

1. When Tzŭ Chang asked the best way to improve his character and to discriminate in what was irrational, the Master said: 'Take conscientiousness and sincerity as your ruling principles, submit also your mind to right conditions, and your character will improve. 2. When you love a man you want him to live, when you hate him you wish he were dead; but you have already wanted him to live and yet again you wish he were dead. This is an instance of the irrational.

3. "Not indeed because of wealth,
But solely because talented." '[5]

Chapter XI

1. When Duke Ching of Ch'i inquired of Confucius the principles of government, 2. Confucius answered saying: 'Let the prince be prince, the minister minister, the father father, and the son son.'

3. 'Excellent!' said the Duke. 'Truly, if the prince be not prince, the

---

[2] Chi Tzŭ-Ch'êng was a high official who disliked the veneer of the times.

[3] Duke Ai of Lu, see II. xix.

[4] Yu Jo = Tzŭ Yu.

[5] A quotation, perhaps meaning that people are not sought out for wealth but talent.

minister not minister, the father not father, and the son not son, however much grain I may have, shall I be allowed to eat it?'[6]

CHAPTER XII

1. The Master said: 'Yu[7] was a fellow! He could decide a dispute with half a word.' 2. Tzŭ Lu never slept over a promise.

CHAPTER XIII

The Master said: 'I can try a lawsuit as well as other men, but surely the great thing is to bring about that there be no going to law.'

CHAPTER XIV

When Tzŭ Chang asked about the art of government, the Master replied: 'Ponder untiringly over your plans, and then conscientiously carry them into execution.'

CHAPTER XV

The Master said: 'The scholar[8] who becomes widely versed in letters, and who restrains his learning within the bounds of good conduct, is not likely to leave the track.'

CHAPTER XVI

The Master said: 'The man of noble mind seeks to achieve the good in others and not their evil. The little-minded man is the reverse of this.'

CHAPTER XVII

When Chi K'ang Tzŭ[9] asked Confucius for a definition of government, Confucius replied: 'To govern means to guide aright. If you, Sir, will lead the way aright, who will dare to deviate from the right?'

---

[6] This occurred in 518 B.C. when Confucius was 35 years old. The duke had lost his government to his ministers, and was surrounded by many concubines through whose jealousies the family relationships were all astray. See XVI. xii and XVIII. iii.

[7] Yu = Tzŭ Lu.

[8] See VI. xxv.

[9] xvii–xix. Chi K'ang Tzŭ, the minister, see xx. Chapter xix is a famous paragraph.

Chapter XVIII

Chi K'ang Tzŭ, being plagued with robbers, consulted Confucius, who answered him saying: 'If you, Sir, be free from the love of wealth, although you pay people, they will not steal.'

Chapter XIX

Chi K'ang Tzŭ asked the opinion of Confucius on government and said: 'How would it do to execute the lawless for the good of the law-abiding?' 'What need, Sir, is there of capital punishment in your administration?' responded Confucius. 'If your aspirations are for good, Sir, the people will be good. The moral character of those in high position is the breeze, the character of those below is the grass. When the grass has the breeze upon it, it assuredly bends.'

Chapter XX

1. Tzŭ Chang asked what a man must be like in order to gain general estimation. 2. 'What is it that you mean by general estimation?' inquired the Master. 3. 'To ensure popularity abroad and to ensure it at home,' replied Tzŭ Chang.

4. 'That,' said the Master, 'is popularity, not esteem. 5. As for the man who meets with general esteem, he is natural, upright, and a lover of justice; he weighs what men say and observes their expression, and his anxiety is to be more lowly than others; and so he ensures esteem abroad, as he ensures it also at home. 6. As to the seeker of popularity, he assumes an air of magnanimity which his actions belie, while his self-assurance knows never a misgiving, and so he ensures popularity abroad, as he also ensures it at home.'

Chapter XXI

1. Once when Fan Ch'ih was rambling along with the Master under the trees at the Rain Altars, he remarked: 'May I venture to ask how one may improve one's character, correct one's personal faults, and discriminate in what is irrational?'

2. 'An excellent question,' rejoined the Master. 3. 'If a man put duty first and success after, will not that improve his character? If he attack his own failings instead of those of others, will he not remedy his personal faults? For a morning's anger to forget his own safety and involve that of his relatives, is not this irrational?'

Chapter XXII

1. Once when Fan Ch'ih asked the meaning of virtue, the Master replied, 'Love your fellow men.' On his asking the meaning of knowledge, the Master said: 'Know your fellow men.'

2. Fan Ch'ih not having comprehended, 3. the Master added: 'By promoting the straight and degrading the crooked you can make even the crooked straight.'

4. Fan Ch'ih withdrew and afterwards meeting Tzŭ Hsia said to him: 'A little while ago, when I had an interview with the Master, and asked for a definition of knowledge, he replied, "By promoting the straight and degrading the crooked you can make even the crooked straight," — what can he have meant?'

5. 'What a rich maxim that is!' replied Tzŭ Hsia. 6. 'When Shun had the empire,[10] he chose from amongst the multitude and promoted Kao Yao, whereupon all who were devoid of virtue disappeared. And when T'ang had the empire, he too chose from amongst the multitude and promoted I Yin, whereupon all who were devoid of virtue disappeared.'

Chapter XXIII

1. On Tzŭ Kung inquiring the duties to a friend, the Master replied: 'Advise him conscientiously and guide him discreetly. If he be unwilling, then cease; do not court humiliation.'

Chapter XXIV

The philosopher Tsêng said: 'The wise man by his culture gathers his friends, and by his friends develops his goodness of character.'

[10] Shun, the early great emperor, and Kao Yao his minister. T'ang was the first emperor of the Shang or Yin dynasty, and I Yin his minister.

VOLUME VII

BOOK XIII

Chiefly Concerning Government

CHAPTER I

1. When Tzŭ Lu asked about the art of government the Master replied: 'Be in advance of people; show them how to work.'

2. On his asking for something more, the Master added: 'Untiringly.'

CHAPTER II

1. When Chung Kung was minister for the House of Chi he asked for advice on the art of government, whereupon the Master said: 'Utilize first and foremost your subordinate officers, overlook their minor errors, and promote those who are worthy and capable.'

2. 'How may I know those who are worthy and capable?' he asked. 'Promote those you do recognize;' was the reply; 'as to those whom you may fail to recognize, is it likely that others will neglect them?'

CHAPTER III

1. 'The Prince of Wei,'[1] said Tzŭ Lu, 'is awaiting you, Sir, to take control of his administration, — what will you undertake first, Sir?'

2. 'The one thing needed,' replied the Master, 'is the correction of terms.'

3. 'Are you as wide of the mark as that, Sir?' said Tzŭ Lu, 'Why this correcting?'

4. 'How uncultivated you are, Yu!' responded the Master. 'A wise man, in regard to what he does not understand, maintains an attitude of reserve. 5. If terms be incorrect, then statements do not accord with facts; and when statements and facts do not accord, then business is not

---

[1] Prince of Wei, see VII. xiv. This famous passage emphasizes the need of exact wording and thought, to achieve even, good government.

properly executed; 6. when business is not properly executed, order and harmony do not flourish; when order and harmony do not flourish, then justice becomes arbitrary; and when justice becomes arbitrary, the people do not know how to move hand or foot. 7. Hence whatever a wise man states he can always define, and what he so defines, he can always carry into practice; for the wise man will on no account have anything remiss in his definitions.'

Chapter IV

1. On Fan Ch'ih requesting to be taught agriculture, the Master replied, 'I am not as good as an old farmer for that.' When he asked to be taught gardening the Master answered, 'I am not as good as an old gardener for that.'

2. On Fan Ch'ih withdrawing, the Master said: 'What a little-minded man is Fan Hsü! 3. When a ruler loves good manners, his people will not let themselves be disrespectful; when a ruler loves justice, his people will not let themselves be unsubmissive; when a ruler loves good faith, his people will not venture to be insincere; — and if he be like this, then people will come from every quarter carrying their children strapped on their backs; — what does he want with learning agriculture?'

Chapter V

The Master said: 'A man may be able to recite the three hundred Odes, but if, when given a post in the administration, he proves to be without practical ability, or when sent anywhere on a mission, he is unable of himself to answer a question, although his knowledge is extensive, of what use is it?'

Chapter VI

The Master said: 'If a ruler is himself upright, his people will do their duty without orders; but if he himself be not upright, although he may order they will not obey.'

Chapter VII

The Master said: 'Lu and Wei are brother states even in their misgovernment.'[2]

---

[2] Said with a sigh, for the states of Lu and Wei, originally brother states, were also brothers in upheaval.

CHAPTER VIII

The Master said of Ching, a scion of the ducal House of Wei, that he dwelt well content in his house. When first he began to possess property, he called it 'a passable accumulation'; when he had prospered somewhat, he called it 'passably complete'; and when he had amassed plenty, he called it 'passably fine'.[3]

CHAPTER IX

1. When the Master was travelling to Wei, Jan Yu drove him. 2. 'What a numerous population!' remarked the Master.

3. 'The people having grown so numerous, what next should be done for them?' asked Jan Yu. 'Enrich them,' was the reply.

4. 'And when you have enriched them, what next should be done?' he asked. 'Educate them,' was the answer.

CHAPTER X

The Master said: 'Were any prince to employ me, in a twelvemonth something could have been done, but in three years the work could be completed.'

CHAPTER XI

The Master remarked: 'How true is the saying: "If good men ruled the country for a hundred years, they could even tame the brutal and abolish capital punishment!" '

CHAPTER XII

The Master said: 'If a kingly ruler were to arise, it would take a generation before virtue prevailed, however.'

CHAPTER XIII

The Master said: 'If a man put himself aright, what difficulty will he have in the public service; but if he cannot put himself aright, how is he going to put others right?'

[3] The Master praised Ching because he was not greedy or proud.

CHAPTER XIV

Once when Jan Tzŭ came from court, the Master asked, 'Why are you so late?' 'We had affairs of state,' was the reply. 'They must have been family affairs, then,' said the Master. 'If there had been affairs of state, although I am not engaged in office, yet I should have been consulted about them.'[4]

CHAPTER XV

1. Duke Ting[5] inquired whether there were any one phrase by the adoption of which a country could be made prosperous. 'No phrase can be expected to have such force as that,' replied Confucius. 2. 'But there is the popular saying, "It is hard to be a prince, and not easy to be a minister." 3. If a prince perceive the difficulty of being a prince, may he not expect through that one phrase to prosper his country?'

4. 'Is there any one phrase,' he asked, 'through which a country may be ruined?' 'No phrase can be expected to have such force as that,' replied Confucius. 'But there is the popular saying, "I should have no gratification in being a prince, unless none opposed my commands." 5. If those are good, and no one opposes them, that surely is well. But if they are not good, and no one opposes them, may he not expect in that one phrase to ruin his country?'

CHAPTER XVI

1. When the Duke of Shê[6] asked the meaning of good government, 2. the Master answered: 'The near are happy and the distant attracted.'

CHAPTER XVII

When Tzŭ Hsia was magistrate of Chü-fu,[7] he asked what should be his policy, whereupon the Master said: 'Do not be in a hurry; do not be intent on minor advantages. When one is in a hurry, nothing is thorough; and when one is intent on minor advantages, nothing great is accomplished.'

---

[4] The Master rebuking Jan Tzŭ, for he himself was entitled to consultation if State affairs were in progress.

[5] Duke Ting, see III. xix.

[6] xvi and xviii. Duke of Shê, see VII. xviii.

[7] A city in the state of Lu.

Chapter XVIII

1. The Duke of Shê observed to Confucius: 'In my part of the country there is a man so honest that when his father appropriated a sheep he bore witness to it.' 2. 'The honest in my part of the country,' replied Confucius, 'are different from that, for a father will screen his son, and a son his father, — and there is honesty in that.'

Chapter XIX

Once when Fan Ch'ih asked about virtue, the Master said: 'In private life be courteous, in handling public business be serious, with all men be conscientious. Even though you go among barbarians, you may not relinquish these virtues.'

Chapter XX

1. Tzŭ Kung asked: 'What must an official be like to merit his name?' 'If in his personal conduct,' replied the Master, 'he has a sensibility to dishonour, and wheresoever he be sent will not disgrace his prince's commission, he may be said to merit his title.'

2. 'I would venture to ask who may be ranked lower,' said Tzŭ Kung. 'He whom his relatives commend as filial and whose neighbours commend as brotherly,' was the answer.

3. 'I venture to ask the next lower,' said Tzŭ Kung. 'He is one who always stands by his word,' was the answer, 'and who persists in all he undertakes; he is a man of grit, though of narrow outlook; yet perhaps he may be taken as of the third class.'

4. 'What would you say of the present-day government officials?' asked Tsŭ Kung. 'Faugh!' said the Master. 'A set of pecks and hampers, unworthy to be taken into account!'

Chapter XXI

The Master said: 'If I cannot obtain men of the Golden Mean to teach, those whom I must have, let them be the ambitious and the discreet; for the ambitious do make progress and take hold, and as to the discreet, there are things that they will refuse to sanction.'

Chapter XXII

1. The Master said: 'The men of the South have a saying: "A man without constancy will make neither a soothsayer nor a doctor." How

well put! 2. The *I Ching* says: "If a man be inconstant in his moral character, some one will bring disgrace upon him." ' 3. The Master remarked: 'All because he did not think well beforehand.'

CHAPTER XXIII

The Master said: 'The true gentleman is friendly but not familiar; the inferior man is familiar but not friendly.'

CHAPTER XXIV

Tzŭ Kung asked: 'What would you say of the man who is liked by all his fellow townsmen?' 'That is not sufficient,' was the reply. 'Then what would you say of him who is hated by all his fellow townsmen?' 'Nor is that sufficient,' was the reply. 'What is better is that the good among his fellow townsmen like him, and the bad hate him.'

CHAPTER XXV

The Master said: 'The true gentleman is easy to serve, yet difficult to please. If you attempt to please him in any improper way, he will be displeased; but when it comes to appointing men in their work, he has regard to their capacity. The inferior man is hard to serve, yet easy to please. If you attempt to please him, even in an improper way, he will be pleased; but in appointing men their work, he expects them to be fit for everything.'

CHAPTER XXVI

The Master said: 'The well-bred are dignified but not pompous. The ill-bred are pompous, but not dignified.'

CHAPTER XXVII

The Master said: 'The firm of spirit, the resolute in character, the simple in manner, and the slow of speech are not far from virtue.'

CHAPTER XXVIII

Tzŭ Lu asked: 'What qualities must one possess to be entitled to be called an educated man?' 'He who is earnest in spirit, persuasive in speech, and withal of gracious bearing,' said the Master, 'may be called an educated man;—earnest in spirit and persuasive of speech with his friends, and of gracious bearing towards his brothers.'

CHAPTER XXIX

The Master said: 'When a good man has trained the people for seven years, they might then be fit to bear arms.'

CHAPTER XXX

The Master said: 'To lead an untrained people to war may be called throwing them away.'

BOOK XIV

Chiefly Concerning Government and Certain Rulers

CHAPTER I

When Hsien[1] asked the meaning of dishonour, the Master said: 'When his country is well-governed to be thinking only of pay, and when his country is ill-governed to be thinking only of pay,—that is dishonour for a man.'

CHAPTER II

1. Hsien again asked: 'If a man refrain from ambition, boasting, resentment, and selfish desire, it may, I suppose, be counted to him for virtue.'
2. 'It may be counted for difficult,' said the Master, 'but whether that alone is virtue, I know not.'

CHAPTER III

The Master said: 'The scholar whose regard is his comfort is unworthy to be deemed a scholar.'

CHAPTER IV

The Master said: 'When law and order prevail in the land, a man may be bold in speech and bold in action; but when the land lacks law and order, though he may take bold action, he should lay restraint on his speech.'

CHAPTER V

The Master said: 'A man of principle is sure to have something good to say, but he who has something good to say is not necessarily a man of

[1] i and ii. Hsien = Yüan Ssŭ, noted for his modesty and purity.

principle. A virtuous man is sure to be courageous, but a courageous man is not necessarily a man of virtue.'

Chapter VI

Nan Kung Kua remarked to Confucius by way of inquiry: 'Is it not a fact that Prince I excelled as an archer, and Ao could propel a boat on dry land, yet neither died a natural death, while Yü and Chi, who took a personal interest in agriculture, became possessed of the empire?' The Master made no reply, but when Nan Kung Kua had withdrawn, he observed: 'A scholar indeed is such a man! Such a man has a true estimation of virtue!'[2]

Chapter VII

'There may perhaps be men of the higher type who fail in virtue, but there has never been one of the lower type who possessed virtue.'

Chapter VIII

The Master said: 'Can love be other than exacting, or loyalty refrain from admonition?'

Chapter IX

The Master said: 'In preparing a state document in Chêng,[3] P'i Shên drafted it, Shih Shu revised it, the Foreign Minister Tzŭ Yü amended it, and Tzŭ Ch'an of Tung Li embellished it.'

Chapter X

1. Somebody asked the Master what he thought about Tzŭ Ch'an: 'He is a kindly man,' was the reply. 2. Asked about Tzŭ Hsi, he said: 'That fellow indeed!' 3. Asked about Kuan Chung, he said: 'There was a man! The head of the Po family was despoiled for him of his town of P'ien with

---

[2] Prince I and Ao, athletes of ancient times. Yü in person and Chi through his posterity, the Chou dynasty, developed the resources of the land in ancient times, and thus became rulers.

[3] Chêng was a small state, needing and receiving the co-operative service of all its officials to survive.

its three hundred families, yet never even complained, though he had to live on coarse food to the end of his days.'[4]

Chapter XI

The Master said: 'To be poor and not complain is difficult; to be rich and not arrogant is easy.'

Chapter XII

The Master said: 'Mêng Kung Ch'o[5] would excel as comptroller of the Chao or Wei families, but is not fit to be minister in the states of T'êng or Hsieh.'

Chapter XIII

1. When Tzŭ Lu asked what constituted the character of the perfect man, the Master replied: 'If he have the sagacity of Tsang Wu Chung, the purity of Kung Ch'o, the courage of Chuang Tzŭ of P'ien, and the skill of Jan Ch'iu, and if he refine these with the arts of courtesy and harmony, then, indeed, he may be deemed a perfect man.'[6]

2. 'But what need is there,' he added, 'for the perfect man of the present day to be like this? Let him when he sees anything to his advantage think whether it be right; when he meets with danger be ready to lay down his life; and, however long-standing the undertaking, let him not belie the professions of his whole life: then he, too, may be deemed a perfect man.'

Chapter XIV

1. The Master put a question to Kung-ming Chia[7] about Kung-shu Wên-tzŭ, and said: 'Is it really true that your Master neither talks, nor laughs, nor accepts anything?'

---

[4] Tzŭ Ch'an was a kindly official but not lenient, see v. xv. Tzŭ Hsi had prevented his prince from employing Confucius.

[5] Mêng Kung Ch'o (see xiii), an official of more probity than talent.

[6] Tsang Wu Chung was a sage of the preceding reign. Kung Ch'o = Mêng Kung Ch'o, of preceding chapter, xii. Chuang Tzŭ of P'ien killed two tigers in one day. Jan Ch'iu is the clever but unscrupulous disciple serving under Chi K'ang Tzŭ in Lu.

[7] Kung-ming Chia was disciple to Kung-shu Wên-tzŭ, an official who was a stoic philosopher.

2. 'That arises from the exaggeration of reporters,' answered Kung-ming Chia. 'Our Master talks only at the right time, hence people do not tire of his talk; he only laughs when he is really pleased, hence people do not tire of his laughter; he only accepts things when it is right to do so, hence men do not tire of his accepting.' 'Is that so?' said the Master. 'Can that indeed be so?'

CHAPTER XV

The Master said: 'Tsang Wu Chung[8] held on to the fief of Fang while he begged the Duke of Lu to appoint his brother as his successor. Although they say he did not coerce his prince, I do not believe it.'

CHAPTER XVI

The Master said: 'Duke Wên of Chin[9] was double-dealing and dishonourable. Duke Huan of Ch'i was honourable and not double-dealing.'

CHAPTER XVII

1. 'When Duke Huan put to death his brother, Prince Chiu,' observed Tzŭ Lu, 'Shao Hu died for him, but Kuan Chung did not. Was he not lacking in virtue?' 2. 'Duke Huan,' answered the Master, 'brought the barons together without resorting to chariots of war, and all through the power of Kuan Chung. Whose virtue was like his? Whose virtue was like his?'[10]

CHAPTER XVIII

1. Tzŭ Kung asked: 'Was not Kuan Chung deficient in virtue? When Duke Huan had his brother Prince Chiu put to death, Kuan Chung was incapable of dying, and even became his minister.'

2. 'After Kuan Chung became minister to Duke Huan,' replied the Master, 'he made the duke leader of the barons, and entirely reduced

---

[8] Tsang Wu Chung, having offended the ruler, fled in disgrace, but kept a hold on the fief of Fang, demanding that his half-brother be appointed to its command.

[9] Duke Wên, 635–627 B.C.: Duke Huan 683–640 B.C. Neither was upright, but Huan was at least not treacherous.

[10] Duke Huan, see above. Shao Hu and Kuan Chung were both ministers of the murdered Prince Chiu. Shao committed suicide in protest, but Kuan Chung asked merely to be imprisoned, later took office under Huan, and acted with so much ability that Confucius praises him. See XIV. X.

the empire to order, so that people down to the present day are recipients of his benefactions. But for Kuan Chung we should be wearing our hair loose and folding our clothes to the left. 3. Would you require from him that which is deemed fidelity by common men and women, who show it by committing suicide in some ditch, nobody being the wiser?'

CHAPTER XIX

1. The Minister Chüan, formerly a retainer of Kung-shu Wen-tzŭ, afterwards went up to court in company with Wen-tzŭ. 2. The Master on hearing of it observed: 'Wen well deserves to be considered "a promoter of culture".'[11]

CHAPTER XX

1. When the Master was speaking of the unprincipled character of Duke Ling of Wei, K'ang-tzŭ[12] observed: 'Such being the case, how is it he does not lose his throne?' 2. 'Chung-shu Yü,' answered Confucius, 'has charge of the envoys; the Reader T'o has charge of the ancestral temple; Wang-sun Chia commands the forces; — and, such being the case, how should he lose his throne?'

CHAPTER XXI

The Master said: 'He who speaks without modesty will perform with difficulty.'

CHAPTER XXII

1. When Ch'ên Ch'êng-tzŭ slew Duke Chien, 2. Confucius bathed himself and went to court, where he petitioned Duke Ai, saying: 'Ch'ên Hêng has slain his prince, I beg you to take vengeance on him.'

3. 'Lay the information before the three nobles,' replied the Duke.

4. 'Seeing that I rank next after the ministers,' soliloquized Confucius (as he withdrew), 'I dare not do other than petition; and the prince says: "Inform the three nobles!" '

5. He went to the three nobles and petitioned them, but they declined

---

[11] Kung-shu Wen-tzŭ, see XIV. xiv. A play on the word *Wên*, which means 'Cultured'.
[12] K'ang-tzŭ = Chi K'ang Tzŭ, the minister in Lu. Duke Ling, though unprincipled, had three excellent ministers to do the work of government.

action; whereupon Confucius remarked: 'Seeing that I rank next after the ministers, I dared not do other than make my petition.'[13]

Chapter XXIII

When Tzŭ Lu asked what constituted a man's duty to his prince, the Master said: 'Never deceive him and then you may boldly withstand him.'

Chapter XXIV

The Master said: 'The progress of the nobler-minded man is upwards, the progress of the inferior man is downwards.'

Chapter XXV

The Master said: 'The men of old studied for the sake of self-improvement; the men of the present day study for the approbation of others.'

Chapter XXVI

1. Chü Po Yü[14] having sent a messenger to convey his respects to Confucius, 2. Confucius made him sit down along with him and questioned him, asking: 'What is your master doing now?' The messenger replied: 'My master is seeking to make his faults fewer, but has not yet succeeded.' When the messenger had withdrawn, the Master observed: 'What a messenger! What a messenger!'

Chapter XXVII

The Master said: 'He who does not occupy the office does not discuss its policy.'[15]

Chapter XXVIII

The Philosopher Tsêng said: 'A wise man, even in his thoughts, does not stray from his own duty.'

---

[13] Ch'ên was minister in the neighbouring state of Ch'i and had slain his duke, Chien, greatly shocking Confucius. He wished Duke Ai to take up arms, but Duke Ai's three chieftains were secretly allies of the murderer, and put Confucius off.

[14] Chü Po Yü, a former disciple, host and sage.

[15] See VIII. xiv.

Chapter XXIX

The Master said: 'The higher type of man is modest in what he says, but surpasses in what he does.'

Chapter XXX

1. The Master said: 'There are three characteristics of the noble man's life, to which I cannot lay claim: — being virtuous he is free from care; possessing knowledge he is free from doubts; being courageous he is free from fear.' 2. 'That is what you say of yourself!' replied Tzŭ Kung.

Chapter XXXI

Tzŭ Kung being in the habit of making comparisons, the Master observed: 'How worthy T'zŭ must be! As for me, I have not the time to spare.'

Chapter XXXII

The Master said: 'A wise man is not distressed that people do not know him; he is distressed at his own lack of ability.'

Chapter XXXIII

The Master said: 'Is not he a man of real worth who does not anticipate deceit nor imagine that people will doubt his word; and yet who has immediate perception thereof when present?'

Chapter XXXIV

1. Wei-shêng Mou,[16] sneering at Confucius, said: 'Ch'iu, what are you doing with this "perching here and perching there"? Are you not making a business of talking to please people?' 2. 'I should not dare to talk only to please people,' replied Confucius; 'and I should hate to be obstinately immovable.'

Chapter XXXV

The Master said: 'A good horse is not praised for its strength but for its character.'

---

[16] Wei-shêng Mou, an aged recluse and moralist, who sneered at Confucius's wandering exile, and teachings.

Chapter XXXVI

1. Some one asked: 'What do you think about the principle of rewarding enmity with kindness?' 2. 'With what, then, would you reward kindness?' asked the Master. 3. 'Reward enmity with just treatment, and kindness with kindness.'

Chapter XXXVII

1. 'No one knows me, alas!' exclaimed the Master. 2. 'Why do you say, Master, that no one knows you?' said Tzŭ Kung. 'I make no complaint against Heaven,' replied the Master, 'nor blame men, for though my studies are lowly, my mind soars aloft; and does not Heaven know me?'

Chapter XXXVIII

1. Kung-po Liao[17] having spoken against Tzŭ Lu to Chi-sun, Tzŭ-fu Ching-po informed Confucius thereof, and said: 'Our lord's mind is undoubtedly being disturbed by Kung-po Liao, but I am still strong enough to have his carcass exposed in the market-place.' 2. The Master replied: 'If my principles are going to prevail, it is so fated; if they are going to fail, it is so fated; what can Kung-po Liao do against Destiny?'

Chapter XXXIX

1. The Master said: 'Some good men withdraw from the world. 2. Withdrawal from fatherland comes next in order; 3. next is from uncongenial looks; 4. and next is from uncongenial language.'

Chapter XL

The Master said: 'There are seven men who have done this.'

Chapter XLI

On one occasion when Tzŭ Lu happened to spend the night at Stone Gate, the gate opener asked him, 'Where are you from?' 'Master

[17] Kung-po Liao, the Duke's uncle, jealous of Tzŭ Lu, who was putting into practice the Master's teachings, spoke against him to their common lord, the minister Chi K'ang Tzŭ, or Chi-sun. Tzŭ-Lu Ching-po, a powerful minister, and a disciple, threatened drastic retaliation.

K'ung's,' replied Tzŭ Lu. 'Is not he the one who knows he cannot succeed and keeps on trying to do so?' was the response.

CHAPTER XLII

1. The Master was playing on a stone chime one day in Wei, when a hermit carrying a basket[18] passed the door of the K'ung abode and remarked: 'With what feeling he is playing the chimes!' 2. Presently he jeered: 'How contemptible is this petrified ting-tinging! Seeing that everybody ignores him, let him stop and have done with it. "If the water is deep you strip up to the waist; if shallow you tuck up your skirt!" ' 3. 'What a stoic he is!' observed the Master. 'But his way is not difficult.'

CHAPTER XLIII

Tzŭ Chang said: 'The *Book of History* says that when Kao Tsung[19] observed the imperial mourning he did not speak for three years. What may be the meaning of that?' 2. 'Why need you specialize Kao Tsung? All the men of old did the same,' answered Confucius. 'When a prince died, all his officers attended to their several duties in obedience to the prime minister for three years.'

CHAPTER XLIV

The Master said: 'When those in high position are fond of orderly behaviour, service from the people is easily commanded.'

CHAPTER XLV

When Tzŭ Lu asked what should be the character of a man of the nobler order, the Master replied: 'He should cultivate himself unfailingly to respect others.' 'Will it suffice to be like this?' asked Tzŭ Lu. 'He should cultivate himself so as to ease the lot of others,' was the reply. 'And is this sufficient?' asked Tzŭ Lu. 'He should cultivate himself so as to ease the lot of the people. He should cultivate himself so as to ease the lot of the people:—even Yao and Shun[20] ever remained assiduous about this!'

---

[18] The basket-carrier, also a recluse, is at first moved by Confucius's music; then jeers that Confucius has not the sense to accommodate himself to the shallowness of the times.

[19] Kao Tsung, Emperor of the Shang dynasty, 1323–1263 B.C.

[20] Yao and Shun, the first great emperors.

CHAPTER XLVI

Yüan Jang[21] sat squatting and waiting as the Master approached, who said to him: 'When young being mannerless, when grown up doing nothing worthy of mention, when old not dying, — this is being a rogue!' And with this he hit him on the shank with his staff.

CHAPTER XLVII

1. A youth from the village of Ch'üeh was acting as messenger for Confucius, so some one said concerning him: 'He has made good progress, I suppose?' 2. 'I notice,' replied the Master, 'that he occupies the seat of adult age, and I notice that he walks on a level with his seniors. It is not that he seeks to progress, he wants speedy arrival!'

[21] Yüan Jang, an old scapegrace.

VOLUME VIII

BOOK XV

Chiefly on the Maintenance of Principles and Character

CHAPTER I

1. When Duke Ling of Wei[1] asked Confucius about military tactics, Confucius replied: 'With the appurtenances of worship I have indeed an acquaintance, but as to military matters I have never studied them.' Next day he straightway took his departure.

2. On the way in Ch'ên their supplies failed, and his followers were so ill that they could not stand. 3. Tzŭ Lu with some irritation sought an interview and said: 'Does a man of the higher order also have to suffer want?' 'The superior man bears want unshaken,' replied the Master, 'the inferior man in want becomes demoralized.'

CHAPTER II

1. 'T'zŭ,' said the Master, 'You regard me as a man of multifarious study who retains all in mind, eh?' 2. 'Yes,' answered he; 'but maybe it is not so?' 3. 'No,' was the reply, 'I have one principle connecting all.'

CHAPTER III

'Yu,' said the Master, 'there are few who understand virtue.'

CHAPTER IV

The Master said: 'May not Shun[2] be instanced as one who made no effort, yet the empire was well governed? For what effort did he make?

---

[1] Duke Ling of Wei, husband of Nan-tzŭ, the dissolute beauty. See XIV. xx. Confucius went to Wei more than once in his exile.

[2] Shun, Emperor, see VIII. xviii.

Ordering himself in all seriousness, he did nothing but maintain the correct imperial attitude.'

CHAPTER V

1. When Tzŭ Chang asked how to succeed with others, 2. the Master made answer: 'If you are sincere and truthful in what you say, and trustworthy and circumspect in what you do, then although you be in the land of the barbarians you will succeed with them. But if you are not sincere and truthful in what you say, and untrustworthy and not circumspect in what you do, are you likely to succeed even in your own country? 3. When standing, see these principles there in front of you. When in your carriage, see them resting on the yoke. Then you will succeed everywhere.' 4. Tzŭ Chang inscribed these counsels on his sash.

CHAPTER VI

1. The Master said: 'What a straight man was the recorder Yü! When the country was well governed, he was like an arrow; and when the country was ill governed, he was still straight as an arrow.

2. What a noble man is Chü Po Yü! When the country is well governed, he holds office; but when the country is ill governed, he can roll up his portfolio and keep it in his bosom.'[3]

CHAPTER VII

'Not to enlighten one who can be enlightened is to waste a man; to enlighten one who cannot be enlightened is to waste words. The intelligent man neither wastes his man nor his words.'

CHAPTER VIII

The Master said: 'The resolute scholar and the virtuous man will not seek life at the expense of virtue. Some even sacrifice their lives to crown their virtue.'

---

[3] In the 'Family Sayings of Confucius', the recorder Yü is said to have been unable to obtain the promotion of good officials and the dismissal of bad. So, when dying, he ordered that his body should be laid out in an unworthy place and state. When his prince saw, he realized the lesson: and Yü accomplished after death what had been impossible to him before. Chü Po Yü, see XIV. xxvi.

Chapter IX

When Tzŭ Kung asked about the practice of virtue, the Master replied: 'A workman who wants to do his work well must first sharpen his tools. In whatever state you dwell, take service with the worthiest of its ministers, and make friends of the most virtuous of its scholars.'

Chapter X

1. Yen Yüan once asked about the administration of a state.
2. The Master replied: 'Adopt the calendar of Hsia;
3. Ride in the state carriage of Yin;
4. Wear the cap of Chou;
5. In music adopt the Shao dances;
6. Banish the songs of Chêng, and avoid specious men; for the songs of Chêng are licentious, and specious men dangerous.'[4]

Chapter XI

The Master said: 'Who heeds not the future will find sorrow at hand.'

Chapter XII

'It is all in vain!' said the Master. 'I have never yet seen a man as fond of virtue as of beauty.'[5]

Chapter XIII

'Was not Tsang Wên Chung like one who had stolen his office?' remarked the Master. 'He knew the excellence of Hui of Liu-hsia, yet did not appoint him as a colleague.'[6]

---

[4] (2) The Calendar of the Hsia dynasty, according to the greatest ancient thought, by beginning at the winter solstice, set forth rightly the harmonious place of heaven, earth, and man, and thus gave right directions for prince and peasant. (3) The state carriage of the Yin dynasty was of simple wood, without trappings. (4) The cap of Chou, with its fringe, was used for sacred rites. (5) The posturings accompanying the ancient Shao music were stately and ordered, see III. xxv. (6) The songs of Chêng were modern and frivolous to the ear of Confucius.

[5] Said when he saw Duke Ling riding out with his wanton wife, Nan-tzŭ.

[6] Tsang Wên Chung, Prime Minister of Lu. Hui of Liu-hsia, an incorruptible judge, see XVIII. ii, viii.

CHAPTER XIV

The Master said: 'He who demands much from himself and little from others will avoid resentment.'

CHAPTER XV

The Master said: 'If a man does not ask himself, "What am I to make of this?" "What am I to make of that?' — there is nothing whatever I can make of him.'

CHAPTER XVI

The Master said: 'Men who associate together the livelong day and whose conversation never rises to what is just and right, but whose delight is in deeds of petty shrewdness — how hard is their case!'

CHAPTER XVII

The Master said: 'The noble man takes the Right as his foundation principle, reduces it to practice with all courtesy, carries it out with modesty, and renders it perfect with sincerity. Such is the noble man.'

CHAPTER XVIII

The Master remarked: 'The noble man is pained over his own incompetency; he is not pained that others ignore him.'

CHAPTER XIX

The Master said: 'The noble man hates to end his days and leave his name undistinguished.'

CHAPTER XX

The Master said: 'The noble man seeks what he wants in himself; the inferior man seeks it from others.'

CHAPTER XXI

The Master said: 'The noble man upholds his dignity without striving for it; he is sociable without entering any clique.'

CHAPTER XXII

The Master said: 'The wise man does not appreciate a man because of what he says; nor does he depreciate what he says because of the man.'

CHAPTER XXIII

'Is there any one word,' asked Tzŭ Kung, 'which could be adopted as a lifelong rule of conduct?' The Master replied: 'Is not Sympathy the word? Do not do to others what you would not like yourself.'

CHAPTER XXIV

1. The Master said: 'In my treatment of men, whom have I unduly disparaged or whom have I unduly extolled? If there be one whom I have so extolled, there is that by which he has been tested. 2. Thus and with such people the Three Dynasties pursued their straightforward course.'

CHAPTER XXV

The Master said: 'I can still go back to the days when a recorder left a temporary blank in his records, and when a man who had a horse would lend it to another to ride. Now, alas! such a condition no more exists.'

CHAPTER XXVI

The Master said: 'Plausible words confound morals, and a trifling impatience may confound a great project.'

CHAPTER XXVII

The Master said: 'Though all hate a man, one must investigate the cause; and though all like him, one must also investigate the cause.'

CHAPTER XXVIII

The Master said: 'A man can enlarge his principles; it is not his principles that enlarge the man.'

CHAPTER XXIX

The Master said: 'To err and not reform may indeed be called error.'

CHAPTER XXX

The Master said: 'I have spent the whole day without food and the whole night without sleep in order to think. It was of no use. It is better to learn.'

CHAPTER XXXI

The Master said: 'The wise man makes duty, not a living, his aim; for there is hunger even for a farmer, and sometimes emolument for a scholar! But the wise man is anxious about his duty, not about poverty.'

CHAPTER XXXII

1. The Master said: 'If a man intellectually realizes a given principle, but if his moral character does not enable him to live up to it, even though he has reached it, he will decline from it. 2. Though intellectually he has attained to it, and his moral character enables him to live up to it, if he does not govern people with dignity, they will not respect him. 3. And though he has intellectually attained to it, his moral character enables him to live up to it, and he governs with dignity, if he instigates the people to act in a disorderly manner, he is still lacking in excellence.'

CHAPTER XXXIII

The Master said: 'A man of the higher type may not be distinguishable in minor responsibilities, but he can undertake great ones. An inferior man cannot undertake great responsibilities, but may be distinguished in minor ones.'

CHAPTER XXXIV

The Master said: 'Virtue is more to man than either water or fire. I have seen men die through walking into water or fire, but I have never seen a man die through walking the path of virtue.'

CHAPTER XXXV

The Master said: 'He upon whom a moral duty devolves should not give way even to his master.'

CHAPTER XXXVI

The Master said: 'The wise man is intelligently, not blindly, loyal.'

CHAPTER XXXVII

The Master said: 'In serving one's prince, one should give careful attention to his business, and make the pay a secondary consideration.'

CHAPTER XXXVIII

The Master said: 'In teaching there should be no class distinctions.'

CHAPTER XXXIX

The Master said: 'Those whose ways are different do not make plans together.'

CHAPTER XL

The Master said: 'In language perspicuity is everything.'

CHAPTER XLI

1. The State Bandmaster Mien[7] once called to see him. On arriving at the steps the Master said, 'Here are the steps.' On coming to the mat, he said, 'Here is your mat.' When all were seated the Master informed him: 'So and so is here, so and so is there.'

2. When the Bandmaster had gone, Tzŭ Chang inquired: 'Is it the proper thing to tell a Bandmaster those things?' 3. 'Yes,' answered the Master, 'undoubtedly it is the proper thing for a blind Bandmaster's guide to do so.'

[7] Musicians in ancient China, as now [1910], were often blind. Confucius treated such with courtesy, both for their art and their disability.

BOOK XVI

Concerning Ministerial Responsibility et Alia

CHAPTER I

1. The chief of the House of Chi[1] being about to invade the minor principality of Chuan-yü, 2. Jan Yu and Chi Lu interviewed Confucius and said: 'Our chief is about to commence operations against Chuan-yü fief.'

3. 'Ch'iu,' said Confucius, 'is not this misdeed yours? 4. The Head of Chuan-yü was appointed by the ancient kings to preside over the sacrifices to the Eastern Mêng; the fief also is within the boundaries of our state, and its ruler is direct sacrificial minister of the crown. What business has your chief with attacking it?'

5. 'It is our master's wish,' said Jan Yu, 'neither of us two ministers wishes it.' 6. 'Ch'iu,' replied Confucius, 'Chou Jen had a saying: "Let him who is allowed to use his ability retain his position, and let him who cannot retire. Of what use is he as a blind man's guide, who neither holds him up when tottering, nor supports him when falling?" 7. Moreover, your remark is quite wrong, for when a tiger or a wild bull escapes from its cage, or when tortoise-shell or a precious stone is injured in its cabinet, whose fault is it?'

8. 'But now,' said Jan Yu, 'Chuan-yü is strongly fortified and near to Pi. If our chief does not take it now it must hereafter become a cause of anxiety to his descendants.'

9. 'Ch'iu,' replied Confucius, 'the man of honour detests those who decline to say plainly that they want a thing and insist on making excuses in regard thereto. 10. I have heard that the ruler of a kingdom, or the chief of a house, is not concerned about his people being few, but about lack of equitable treatment; nor is he concerned over poverty, but over the presence of discontent; for where there is equity there is no poverty,

[1] The disciples Jan Ch'iu and Tzŭ Lu were in the service of the Chief of Chi, who was now planning to attack a small buffer town, being greedy for its sacrificial revenues. The Master plainly tells them that they cannot shelve their responsibility and dissociate themselves from their Chief.

where concord prevails there is no lack of people, and where contentment reigns there are no upheavals. 11. Such a state of things existing, then, if any outlying people are still unsubmissive he attracts them by the promotion of culture and morality, and when he has attracted them he makes them contented. 12. But here are you two, Yu and Ch'iu, assisting your chief; for though an outlying people are unsubmissive, he cannot attract them; and though the state is disorganized and disrupted, he cannot preserve it. 13. And yet he is planning to take up arms within his own state. I myself fear that Chi-sun's cause for anxiety does not lie in Chuan-yü, but within his own gate-screen!'

CHAPTER II

Confucius said: 'When good government prevails in the empire, civil ordinances and punitive expeditions issue from the emperor. When good government fails in the empire, civil ordinances and punitive expeditions issue from the nobles. When they issue from a noble, it is rare if the empire be not lost within ten generations. When they issue from a noble's minister, it is rare if the empire be not lost within five generations. But when a minister's minister holds command in the kingdom, it is rare if it be not lost within three generations. 2. When there is good government in the empire, its policy is not in the hands of ministers. 3. And when there is good government in the empire, the people do not even discuss it.'

CHAPTER III

Confucius said: 'The revenue has departed from the ducal house[2] for five generations, and the government has devolved on ministers for four generations. That, alas! is why the descendants of the three brothers Huan[3] are so reduced!'

CHAPTER IV

Confucius said: 'There are three kinds of friends that are beneficial, and three that are harmful. To make friends with the upright, with the faithful, with the well-informed, is beneficial. To make friends with the plausible, with the insinuating, with the glib, is harmful.'

---

[2] A concrete example of the principle of the preceding paragraph: and a description of the times.

[3] Huan, see XIV. xvi.

CHAPTER V

Confucius said: 'There are three ways of pleasure-seeking that are beneficial, and there are three that are harmful. To seek pleasure in the refinements of manners and music, to seek pleasure in discussing the excellences of others, to seek pleasure in making many worthy friends — these are beneficial. To seek pleasure in unbridled enjoyment, to seek pleasure in looseness and gadding, to seek pleasure in conviviality — these are harmful.'

CHAPTER VI

Confucius said: 'There are three errors to be avoided when in the presence of a superior: to speak before being called upon, which may be termed forwardness; not to speak when called upon, which may be termed timidity; and to speak before noting a superior's expression, which may be called blindness.'

CHAPTER VII

Confucius said: 'There are three things the nobler type of man is on his guard against. In the period of youth, before his physical nature has settled down, he guards against lust. Having reached his prime, when his physical nature has now attained its mature strength, he guards against combativeness. When he has reached old age, and his physical nature is already decaying, he guards against acquisitiveness.'

CHAPTER VIII

1. Confucius said: 'The man of noble mind holds three things in awe. He holds the Divine Will in awe; he holds the great in awe; and he holds the precepts of the sages in awe. 2. The baser man, not knowing the Divine Will, does not stand in awe of it; he takes liberties with the great; and makes a mock of the precepts of the sages.'

CHAPTER IX

Confucius said: 'Those who have innate wisdom take highest rank. Those who acquire it by study rank next. Those who learn despite natural limitations come next. But those who are of limited ability and yet will not learn — these form the lowest class of men.'

CHAPTER X

Confucius said: 'The wise man has nine points of thoughtful care. In looking, his care is to observe distinctly; in listening, his care is to apprehend clearly; in his appearance, his care is to be kindly; in his manner, his care is to be courteous; in speaking, his care is to be conscientious; in his duties, his care is to be earnest; in doubt, his care is to seek information; in anger, he has a care for the consequences; and when he has opportunity for gain, his care is whether it be right.'

CHAPTER XI

1. Confucius said: ' "They look up at the good as if fearing not to reach it, and shrink from evil as if from scalding water." I have seen such men, as I have heard such sayings. 2. "They dwell in seclusion to think out their aims, and practise right living in order to extend their principles"—I have heard such sayings, but I have never seen such men.'

CHAPTER XII

1. Duke Ching of Ch'i[4] had a team of a thousand horses, but on the day of his death, his people knew of no virtue for which to praise him. Po-I and Shu-Ch'i starved to death at the foot of Mount Shou-Yang, and down to the present the people still praise them. 2. Does not that illustrate this?

CHAPTER XIII

1. Ch'ên K'ang once asked Po Yü:[5] 'Have you ever had any lesson different from the rest of us from the Master?'

2. 'No,' was the reply, 'but he was once standing alone, and as I hastened across the hall, he remarked: "Have you studied the Odes?" "No," I replied. "If you do not study the Odes," he said, "you will have nothing to use in conversation." On going out I set myself to study the Odes. 3. Another day, he was again standing alone, and as I hastened across the hall, he asked: "Have you studied the Rules of Ceremony?" "No," I replied. "If you do not study the Ceremonies, you will have no grounding." On going out I set myself to study the Ceremonies. 4. These are the two lessons I have received.'

---

[4] Duke Ching of Ch'i, see XII. xi and XVIII. iii.

[5] Po Yü, Confucius's son.

5. When Ch'ên K'ang came away he remarked with delight, 'I asked one thing and obtained three—I have learnt about the Odes, I have learnt about the Ceremonies, and I have learnt that the Wise Man keeps his son at a distance.'

CHAPTER XIV

The wife of the prince of a state is called by the prince himself 'Fu-jên'. The Fu-jên calls herself 'Hsia T'ung'. The people of the state call her 'Chün Fu-jên'. When speaking of her to one of another state they call her 'Kua Hsiao Chün'; but one of another state would also call her 'Chün Fu-jên'.[6]

[6] This may be an ancient interpolation, or Confucius may have said it to rectify some disorder. Fu-jên = Consort. The princess calls herself Hsia T'ung, or The Handmaid. Her own people call her The Prince's Consort: but when speaking to those from other states, politely say Our Unworthy Prince's Consort. These others would, however, speak of her as Prince's Consort.

VOLUME IX

BOOK XVII

Recording Unsuitable Calls and Sundry Maxims

CHAPTER I

1. Yang Huo[1] wanted to see Confucius but Confucius would not go to see him, so he sent Confucius a present of a sucking pig. Confucius, timing his visit when the other would be out, went to tender his acknowledgements, but met him on the way. 2. 'Come,' he said to Confucius, 'let me have a word with you. If a man,' he said, 'hide his talent in his bosom, and thus share in his country's misguidance, can he be called a lover of his fellow men?' 'He cannot,' was the reply. 'If a man who would like to take part in public affairs is continually losing his opportunity, can he be called wise?' 'He cannot,' was the reply. 'Days and months are passing by, the years do not wait for us.' 'That is so,' said Confucius, 'I will take office presently.'

CHAPTER II

The Master said: 'By nature men nearly resemble each other; in practice they grow wide apart.'

CHAPTER III

The Master said: 'It is only the very wisest and the very stupidest who never change.'

CHAPTER IV

1. When the Master arrived at Wu city, he heard everywhere the sound of stringed instruments and singing; whereupon he smiled and

[1] Yang Huo, usurping servant, Comptroller to the House of Chi, could not persuade Confucius to do other than decline politely any association with him.

laughingly said, 'Why use a cleaver to kill a chicken?' 3. 'A while ago, Sir,' replied Tzŭ Yu, 'I heard you say: "When men of rank have learnt wisdom they love their fellow men; and when the common people have learnt wisdom they are easily commanded".' 4. 'My disciples!' said the Master, 'Yen's remark is right. What I said before was only in jest.'[2]

Chapter V

1. When Kung-shan Fu-jao[3] was holding Pi in revolt against the House of Chi, he sent for the Master, who was inclined to go to him. 2. But Tzŭ Lu was displeased, and said: 'Verily there is nowhere at all to go; why then must you think of going to Kung-shan?' 3. 'Here is one calling me, and can he be doing it for nothing?' answered the Master. 'If one be willing to employ me, may I not make an eastern Chou of his state?'

Chapter VI

Tzŭ Chang asked Confucius the meaning of virtue, to which Confucius replied: 'To be able everywhere one goes to carry five things into practice constitutes Virtue.' On begging to know what they were, he was told: 'They are courtesy, magnanimity, sincerity, earnestness, and kindness. With courtesy you will avoid insult, with magnanimity you will win all, with sincerity men will trust you, with earnestness you will have success, and with kindness you will be well fitted to command others.'

Chapter VII

1. Pi Hsi[4] sent a formal invitation and the Master was inclined to go. 2. But Tzŭ Lu observed: 'Once upon a time, I heard you say, Sir, "With the man who is personally engaged in a wrongful enterprise, the man of honour declines to associate." Pi Hsi is holding Chung-mou in revolt, what will it be like, Sir, if you go there?'

3. 'True,' said the Master, 'I did use those words; but is it not said of the really hard, that you may grind it and it will not grind down; also is it not said of the really white, that you may dye it but it will not turn black? 4. Am I indeed a bitter gourd? Must I, like it, be hung up and never eaten?'

---

[2] See VI. xii. Tzŭ Yu, or Yen Yen, was administrator at Wu-ch'eng, and had taken great pains to practise the Master's principles of government. He misunderstands the Master's jesting at his over-hard work.

[3] Kung-shan Fu-jao, minister to the Chi House, had imprisoned the head of that family, seizing the fief of Pi.

[4] Pi Hsi, minister of Chin state.

CHAPTER VIII

1. The Master said: 'Yu, have you ever heard of the six good words and the six things that obscure them?' 'Never,' was the reply. 2. 'Sit down then, and I will tell you.' 3. 'Love of kindness, without a love to learn, finds itself obscured by foolishness. Love of knowledge, without a love to learn, finds itself obscured by loose speculation. Love of honesty, without a love to learn, finds itself obscured by harmful candour. Love of straightforwardness, without a love to learn, finds itself obscured by misdirected judgement. Love of daring, without a love to learn, finds itself obscured by insubordination. And love for strength of character, without a love to learn, finds itself obscured by intractability.'

CHAPTER IX

1. The Master said: 'My sons, my disciples, why do you not study the poets? 2. Poetry is able to stimulate the mind, 3. it can train to observation, 4. it can encourage social intercourse, 5. it can modify the vexations of life; 6. from it the student learns to fulfil his more immediate duty to his parents, and his remoter duty to his prince; 7. and in it he may become widely acquainted with the names of birds and beasts, plants and trees.'

CHAPTER X

The Master said to his son Po Yü: 'Have you studied the Chou Nan and the Chao Nan? Is not the man who does not study the Chou Nan and the Chao Nan Odes[5] like one who stands with his face hard up against a wall, eh?'

CHAPTER XI

The Master said: ' "Offerings!" they say, "Offerings!" Can mere gems and silk be called offerings? "Music!" they say, "Music!" Can mere bells and drums be called music?'

CHAPTER XII

The Master said: 'He who shams a stern appearance while inwardly he is a weakling, can only be compared with the vulgar and low; indeed is he not like the thief who sneaks through or skulks over walls?'

[5] The Chou Nan and the Chao Nan, the two first books in *The Odes*, dealing with self-culture and the regulation of the family.

Chapter XIII

The Master said: 'Your honest countryman is the spoiler of morals.'[6]

Chapter XIV

The Master said: 'To proclaim on the road what you hear on the way is virtue thrown away.'

Chapter XV

1. 'These servile fellows!' said the Master. 'How is it possible to serve one's prince along with them? 2. Before obtaining their position they are in anxiety to obtain it, and when they have it they are in anxiety lest they lose it; 3. and if men are in anxiety about losing their position, there is no length to which they will not go.'

Chapter XVI

1. 'In olden times,' said the Master, 'the people had three faults, which nowadays perhaps no longer exist. 2. High spirit in olden times meant liberty in detail; the high spirit of to-day means utter looseness. Dignity of old meant reserve; dignity to-day means resentment and offence. Simple-mindedness of old meant straightforwardness; simple-mindedness to-day is nothing but a mask for cunning.'

Chapter XVII

The Master said: 'Artful address and an insinuating demeanour seldom accompany virtue.'

Chapter XVIII

The Master said: 'I hate the way in which purple robs red of its lustre; I hate the way the airs of Chêng[7] pervert correct music; and I hate the way in which sharp tongues overthrow both states and families.'

Chapter XIX

1. 'I wish I could do without speaking,' said the Master. 2. 'If you did not speak, Sir,' said Tzŭ Kung, 'what should we disciples pass on to others?'

---

[6] Because he hates any change.

[7] See XV. x.

3. 'What speech has Heaven?' replied the Master. 'The four seasons run their courses and all things flourish; yet what speech has Heaven?'

Chapter XX

Ju Pei[8] wished to see Confucius, who excused himself on the ground of sickness; but when the messenger had gone out at the door, he took up his harpsichord and began to sing, so that Ju Pei might hear it.

Chapter XXI

1. Tsai Wo, asking about the three years' mourning, suggested that one year was long enough. 2. 'If,' said he, 'a well-bred man be three years without exercising his manners, his manners will certainly degenerate; and if for three years he make no use of music, his music will certainly go to ruin. 3. In one year the last year's grain is finished and the new grain has been garnered, the seasonal friction-sticks have made their varying fires, — a year would be enough.'

4. 'Would you, then, feel at ease in eating good rice and wearing fine clothes?' asked the Master. 'I should,' was the reply.

5. 'If you would feel at ease, then do so; but a well-bred man, when mourning, does not relish good food when he eats it, does not enjoy music when he hears it, and does not feel at ease when in a comfortable dwelling; therefore he avoids those things. But now you would feel at ease, so go and do them.'

6. When Tsai had gone out, the Master said: 'The unfeelingness of Tsai Yü! Only when a child is three years old does it leave its parents' arms, and the three years' mourning is the universal mourning everywhere. And Yü, — was not he the object of his parents' affection for three years?'

Chapter XXII

The Master said: 'How hard is the case of the man who stuffs himself with food the livelong day, never applying his mind to anything! Are there no checkers or chess to play? Even to do that is surely better than nothing at all.'

Chapter XXIII

Tzŭ Lu once asked: 'Does a man of the nobler class hold courage in estimation?' 'Men of the nobler class,' said the Master, 'deem rectitude

[8] Ju Pei, a former disciple who had offended.

the highest thing. It is men of the nobler class, with courage but without rectitude, who rebel. It is men of the lower order, with courage but without rectitude, who become robbers.'

CHAPTER XXIV

1. 'Do men of the nobler class detest others?' asked Tzŭ Kung. 'They do detest others,' answered the Master. 'They detest men who divulge other people's misdeeds. They detest those low, base people who slander their superiors. They detest the bold and mannerless. They detest the persistently forward who are yet obtuse. 2. And have you, T'zŭ, those whom you detest?' he asked. 'I detest those who count prying out information as wisdom. I detest those who count absence of modesty as courage. I detest those who count denouncing a man's private affairs as straightforwardness,' replied Tzŭ Kung.

CHAPTER XXV

The Master said: 'Of all people, maids and servants are hardest to keep in your house. If you are friendly with them they lose their deference; if you are reserved with them they resent it.'

CHAPTER XXVI

The Master said: 'If a man reach forty and yet be disliked by his fellows, he will be so to the end.'

BOOK XVIII

Concerning Ancient Worthies

CHAPTER I

1. The viscount of Wei withdrew from serving the tyrant Chou; the viscount of Chi was made a slave; Pi Kan remonstrated with the tyrant and suffered death. 2. The Master said: 'The Yin Dynasty thus had three men of virtue.'[1]

CHAPTER II

Hui of Liu-hsia[2] filled the office of Chief Criminal Judge, but had been repeatedly dismissed, and people said to him, 'Is it not time, sir, for you to be going elsewhere?' 'If I do honest public service,' said he, 'where shall I go and not be often dismissed? And if I am willing to do dishonest public service, what need is there for me to leave the land of my parents?'

CHAPTER III

Duke Ching of Ch'i, speaking of how he should receive Confucius, said: 'I cannot receive him on an equality with the chief of the Chi house; I will receive him in a style between the lords of Chi and Mêng.' 'But,' he resumed, 'I am old, and cannot make use of him.' Confucius departed.[3]

---

[1] Period of Chou, the last of the Yin emperors, 1153–1122 B.C. Viscount of Wei was the tyrant's step-brother by a concubine. Chi and Pi Kan were his uncles. All remonstrated with him and suffered. The tyrant tore out Pi Kan's heart that he might see a sage's heart.

[2] See XV. xiii.

[3] See XII. xi. Confucius departed, not because of any lack of honour, for the proposed treatment midway between Chi and Mêng was honourable: but because Duke Chi was too old to reform his government. *Circ.* 516 B.C.

CHAPTER IV

The men of Ch'i sent to Lu a present of a troupe of female musicians,[4] whom Chi Huan Tzŭ accepted, and for three days no Court was held, whereupon Confucius took his departure.

CHAPTER V

1. Chieh Yü,[5] an eccentric man of Ch'u, one day came singing past Confucius' carriage, saying. 'Oh, Phoenix! Oh, Phoenix! What a fall is here! As to the past, reproof is useless, but the future may still be overtaken. Desist! Desist! Great is the peril of those who now fill office.'

2. Confucius alighted, desiring to speak to him, but he hurriedly avoided the Sage. So he had no chance of a talk with him.

CHAPTER VI

1. Ch'ang Chü and Chieh Ni[6] were cultivating their land together when Confucius was passing that way, so he sent Tzŭ Lu to inquire for the ford.

2. 'And who is that holding the reins in the carriage?' asked Ch'ang Chü. 'It is K'ung Ch'iu,' replied Tzŭ Lu. 'Is it K'ung Ch'iu of Lu?' he asked. 'It is,' was the reply. 'Then he knows the ford,' said he.

3. Tzŭ Lu then questioned Chieh Ni. 'Who are you, sir?' asked Chieh Ni. 'I am Chung Yu,' was the answer. 'Are you a disciple of K'ung Ch'iu of Lu?' 'Yes,' replied he. 'All the world is rushing headlong like a swelling torrent and who will help you to remedy it?' he asked. 'As for you, instead of following a leader who flees from one after another, had you not better follow those who flee the world entirely?' With this he fell to raking in his seed without a pause.

4. Tzŭ Lu went off and reported to his Master what they said, who remarked with surprise: 'I cannot herd with birds and beasts; if I may not associate with mankind, with whom then am I to associate? Did right rule prevail in the world, I should not be taking part in reforming it.'

---

[4] The famous incident when Confucius was eclipsed by the eighty courtesans. Chi Huan, minister to Duke Ting, persuaded Ting to accept them.

[5] A recluse.

[6] Two other recluses. K'ung Ch'iu = Confucius. Chung Yu = Tzŭ Lu.

Chapter VII

1. Once when Tzŭ Lu was following the Master on a journey he happened to fall behind. Meeting an old man carrying a basket on his staff, Tzŭ Lu asked him, 'Have you seen my Master, sir?' 'You,' said the old man, 'whose four limbs know not toil, and who cannot distinguish the five grains, who may your Master be?' With that he planted his staff in the ground and commenced weeding.[7]

2. Tzŭ Lu joined his hands together in salutation and stood waiting. 3. The old man kept Tzŭ Lu for the night, killed a fowl, prepared millet, and gave him to eat, introducing also his two sons.

4. Next morning Tzŭ Lu went his way and reported his adventure. 'He is a recluse,' said the Master, and sent Tzŭ Lu back again to see him, but on his arrival the old man had gone. 5. Whereupon Tzŭ Lu said to the sons: 'It is not right to refuse to serve one's country. If the regulations between old and young in family life may not be set aside, how is it that your father sets aside the duty between a prince and his ministers? In his desire to maintain his own personal purity, he subverts one of the main principles of society. A wise man, in whatever office he occupies, fulfils its proper duties, even though he is well aware that right principles have ceased to make progress.'

Chapter VIII

1. The men noted for withdrawal into private life were Po I, Shu Ch'i, Yü Chung, Yi Yi, Chu Chiang, Hui of Liu-hsia, and Shao Lien.[8]

2. The Master observed: 'Those of them who would neither abate their high purpose, nor abase themselves, it seems to me were Po I and Shu Ch'i. 3. Concerning Hui of Liu-hsia and Shao Lien, while they abated their high purpose and abased themselves, what they said made for social order, and what they did hit the mark of what men were anxious about: and that is all. 4. Concerning Yü Chung and Yi Yi, though in their seclusion they were immoderate in their utterances, yet they sustained their personal purity, and their self-immolation had weighty purpose.

---

[7] Another recluse. The five grains: rice, millet, wheat, &c.

[8] Po I and Shu Ch'i, see V. xxii. Yü Chung was the younger brother of T'ai Po, VII. i. He cut off his hair, tattooed his body like the natives among whom he went to dwell, and considered nakedness an adornment. Of Yi Yi and Chu Chiang nothing is known. Hui of Liu-hsia is the incorruptible judge of XV. xiii. Shao Lien was a man of the 'Eastern barbarians' who admirably performed his mourning rites.

5. 'But I am different from these. With me there is no inflexible "thou shalt" or "thou shalt not".'

CHAPTER IX

1. The Bandmaster Chih migrated to Ch'i; 2. Kan, the band-leader of the second repast, migrated to Ch'u; Liao of the third repast to Ts'ai; while Ch'üeh of the fourth repast migrated to Ch'in. 3. The big drummer Fang Shu penetrated to the north of the River; 4. the kettledrummer Wu penetrated to the river Han; 5. while Yang, the assistant master, and Hsiang, the player on the stone chime, penetrated to an island in the sea.[9]

CHAPTER X

The Duke of Chou[10] addressing his son, the Duke of Lu, said: 'The wise prince does not neglect his relatives; nor does he cause his chief ministers to be discontented at his not employing them; he does not dismiss old servants from office without some grave cause for it; nor does he expect one man to be capable of everything.'

CHAPTER XI

The Chou Dynasty possessed the eight valiant men, Po Ta, Po Kua; Chung T'u, Chung Hu; Shu Yeh, Shu Hsia; Chi Sui and Chi Wa.[11]

[9] The eight honourable court musicians left Lu state on its degeneration, going as far as the islands at sea. The 'River' is the Yellow River, which seemed a great distance in those days. The duke had four meals a day and possibly appropriate music at each repast.

[10] The Duke of Chou was regent for his son, the Duke of Lu, and this saying of his is said to have been traditional in Lu.

[11] Eight valiant men of old, said to have been brothers, sons of one mother, born as four sets of twins, as is seen by the pairs of names.

VOLUME X

BOOK XIX

Recorded Sayings of Some Disciples[1]

CHAPTER I

Tzŭ Chang said: 'A servant of the State, who in the presence of danger offers his life, whose first thought in presence of personal gain is whether it be right, whose first thought in sacrifice is reverence, and whose first thought in mourning is grief—he commands approval.'

CHAPTER II

Tzŭ Chang said: 'If a man possess virtue without its enlarging him, if he believe in truth but without steadfastness, how can you tell whether he has these qualities or not?'

CHAPTER III

The disciples of Tzŭ Hsia asked Tzŭ Chang[2] concerning friendship. 'What does Tzŭ Hsia say?' he inquired. 'Tzŭ Hsia says,' they replied, 'If a man be suitable, associate with him, if he be unsuitable, turn him away.' 'This is different from what I have been taught,' said Tzŭ Chang. 'A wise man honours the worthy and tolerates all; he commends the good and commiserates the incompetent. Am I a man of exceptional worth? Then whom among men may I not tolerate? Am I not a man of worth? Then others would be turning me away. Why should there be this turning of others away then?'

---

[1] Recorded Sayings of Some Disciples. 'This book records sayings of the disciples, chiefly those of Tzŭ Hsia and next those of Tzŭ Kung. For in the school of Confucius, after Yen Tzŭ no one equalled Tzŭ Kung in acumen, and after Tsêng Tzŭ none equalled Tzŭ Hsia in sincerity.' Chu Tzŭ's commentary.

[2] Tzŭ Chang was noted for his modesty, Tzŭ Hsia for his precise scholarship.

Chapter IV

Tzŭ Hsia said: 'Even the inferior arts certainly have their attraction; but to go far into them involves a risk of their becoming a hindrance to progress: so the wise man lets them alone.'

Chapter V

Tzŭ Hsia said: 'He who day by day finds out where he is deficient, and who month by month never forgets that in which he has become proficient, may truly be called a lover of learning.'

Chapter VI

Tzŭ Hsia said: 'Broad culture and a steady will, earnest investigation and personal reflection, — virtue is to be found therein.'

Chapter VII

Tzŭ Hsia said: 'As the various craftsmen dwell in their workshops that they may do their work effectively, so the Wise Man applies himself to study that he may carry his wisdom to perfection.'

Chapter VIII

Tzŭ Hsia said: 'The inferior man always embellishes his mistakes.'

Chapter IX

Tzŭ Hsia said: 'The Wise Man varies from three aspects. Seen from a distance he appears stern; when approached he proves gracious; as you listen to him you find him decided in opinion.'

Chapter X

Tzŭ Hsia said: 'The Wise Man obtains the people's confidence before imposing burdens on them, for without confidence they will think themselves oppressed. He also obtains the confidence of his prince before pointing out his errors, for before obtaining such confidence his prince would deem himself aspersed.'

CHAPTER XI

Tzŭ Hsia said: 'He who does not overstep the threshold in the major virtues, may have liberty of egress and ingress in the minor ones.'

CHAPTER XII

1. Tzŭ Yu remarked: 'Tzŭ Hsia's disciples and scholars in sprinkling and sweeping floors, in answering calls and replying to questions, and in advancing and retiring are right enough; but these are the minor branches of education. What is their use when radical principles are absent?'

2. When Tzŭ Hsia heard of it he said: 'Ah! Yen Yu is indeed astray. What is there in the wise man's teaching that is of first importance for propagation, and what is there that is secondary and may be neglected? Disciples are just like the various species of plants, which are classified so as to distinguish them. For can the wise man allow his teaching to befool his disciples? Moreover does any one but a Sage embrace in himself the whole beginning and end of learning?'

CHAPTER XIII

Tzŭ Hsia said: 'The occupant of office when his duties are finished should betake himself to study; and the student when his studies are finished should betake himself to office.'

CHAPTER XIV

Tzŭ Yu observed: 'In mourning let grief suffice as its highest expression.'

CHAPTER XV

Tzŭ Yu remarked: 'My friend Chang[3] does things hardly possible to others, but he is not yet perfect in virtue.'

CHAPTER XVI

Tsêng Tzŭ said: 'What a stately manner Chang puts on! It must be hard to live the perfect life alongside him.'

[3] Chang = Tzŭ Chang.

CHAPTER XVII

Tsêng Tzŭ said: 'I have heard the Master say: "Though a man may never before have shown what was in him, surely he will do so when he mourns his parents." '

CHAPTER XVIII

Tsêng Tzŭ said: 'I have heard the Master observe that the filial piety of Mêng Chuang Tzŭ[4] might in other particulars be possible to other men, but his unaltered maintenance of his father's servants, and of his father's administration,—these they would hardly find possible.'

CHAPTER XIX

When the Chief of the Mêng family appointed Yang Fu as chief criminal judge, the latter came to ask advice of Tsêng Tzŭ who replied: 'The rulers have lost their principles, and for long the people have been disorganized; hence, when you discover evidence against a man, be grieved for and commiserate him and take no pleasure in your discovery.'

CHAPTER XX

Tzŭ Kung said: 'Even the iniquity of Chou[5] was not as extreme as is stated. That is why the wise man abhors to dwell in the swamp, where all the evil of the world flows in.'

CHAPTER XXI

Tzŭ Kung said: 'The transgressions of the Wise Man are like eclipses of the sun or moon. When he transgresses all men look at him. When he recovers all men look up to him.'

CHAPTER XXII

1. Kung-sun Ch'ao[6] of Wei once inquired of Tzŭ Kung: 'From whom did Chung Ni get his learning?' 2. 'The doctrines of Wên and Wu have

---

[4] xviii and xix. Mêng Chuang Tzŭ, a minister of Lu, retained his father's servants after he died, though some were unworthy: and his father's administration, though some of it mistaken. Yang Fu was a disciple of Tsêng Tzŭ, the disciple of Confucius.

[5] The tyrant Chou, last of the Yin dynasty, see XVIII. i.

[6] Kung-sun Ch'ao, the Duke of Wei's grandson, a young courtier. Chung Ni = Confucius.

never yet fallen to the ground,' replied Tzŭ Kung, 'but have remained amongst men. Gifted men have kept in mind their nobler principles, while others not so gifted have kept in mind the minor, so that nowhere have the doctrines of Wên and Wu been absent. From whom then could our Master not learn? And, moreover, what need was there for him to have a regular teacher?'

CHAPTER XXIII

1. Shu-sun Wu-shu,[7] talking to the high officers at Court, remarked: 'Tzŭ Kung is a superior man to Chung Ni.' 2. Tzŭ-fu Ching-po took and told this to Tzŭ Kung, who replied: 'One might illustrate the position with the boundary wall of a building. As to my wall, it only reaches to the shoulder, and with a peep you may see whatever is of value in the house and home. 3. The Master's wall rises fathoms high, and unless you find the gate and go inside, you cannot see the beauties of the temple and the richness of its host of officers. 4. But those who find the gate perhaps are few,—indeed does not His Honour's remark confirm this view?'

CHAPTER XXIV

Shu-sun Wu-shu, having spoken disparagingly of Chung Ni, Tzŭ Kung observed: 'There is no use in doing that, for Chung Ni cannot be disparaged. The excellences of others are mounds and hillocks, which may nevertheless be climbed over, but Chung Ni! He is the sun, the moon, which there is no way of climbing over; and though a man may desire to cut himself off from them, what harm does he do to the sun or moon? He only shows that he has no idea of proportion.'

CHAPTER XXV

1. Ch'ên Tzŭ Ch'in once said to Tzŭ Kung: 'You are too modest, Sir. How can Chung Ni be considered superior to you?'[8] 2. 'An educated man,' replied Tzŭ Kung, 'for a single expression is often deemed wise, and for a single expression is often deemed foolish; hence one should not be heedless in what one says. 3. The impossibility of equalling our

---

[7] xxiii and xxiv. Shu-sun Wu-shu, a high officer of Lu, mentioned rather unfavourably in *The Family Sayings*.

[8] Tzŭ Kung denied energetically any superiority to Confucius (Chung Ni).

Master is like the impossibility of scaling a ladder and ascending to the skies. 4. Were our Master to obtain control of a country, then, as has been said, "He raises his people and they stand; he leads them, and they follow; he gives them tranquillity and multitudes resort to him; he brings his influence to bear on them and they live in harmony; his life is glorious and his death bewailed,"—how is it possible for him to be equalled?'

BOOK XX[1]

Concerning Right Government

CHAPTER I

1. Yao said: 'O, thou Shun! The celestial lineage rests in thy person. Faithfully hold to the golden mean. Should the land become lean, Heaven's bounties will forever end towards you.' 2. And Shun in like terms charged Yü.[2]

3. T'ang said: 'I thy child Li, Dare to use a black ox, And dare clearly to state to Thee, O Most August and Sovereign God, That the sinner I dare not spare, Nor keep Thy ministers, O God, in obscurity, As Thy heart, O God, discerns. If I have sinned, Let it not concern the country; If my country has sinned, Let the sin rest on me.'[3]

4. Wu of Chou conferred great largesses, the good being enriched. 5. 'Although,' said he, 'the tyrant Chou had his host of princes closely related to the throne, they compared not with my men of virtue; and it is upon me that the grievances of the people fell.'[4]

6. He paid careful attention to the weights and measures, revised the laws and regulations, restored the disused offices; and universal government prevailed.

7. He re-established states that had been extinguished, restored the lines of broken succession, called to office men who had exiled themselves; and all the people gave him their hearts. 8. What he laid stress on were the people's food, mourning for the dead, and sacrifices. 9. By his magnanimity he won all, by his good faith he gained the people's confidence, by his diligence he achieved his ends, and by his justice all were gratified.

---

[1] This book consists of three chapters. The first chiefly contains sayings of the great dynastic founders quoted from the Book of History, *Shû Ching*; the second giving Confucius's ideas on government; the third an aphorism by him.

[2] Yao, Shun, Yü, the first emperors.

[3] T'ang, 1765–1752 B.C., who founded the Shang dynasty.

[4] Wu = King Wu the Good, who overthrew the Chou dynasty.

CHAPTER II

1. Tzŭ Chang inquired of Confucius, saying, 'How should a man act to achieve the proper administration of government?' The Master replied: 'Let him honour the five good and banish the four bad rules; then he will be a worthy administrator.' 'What is meant by the five good rules?' asked Tzŭ Chang. 'That the ruler,' replied the Master, 'be beneficent without expending the public revenue, that he exact service without arousing dissatisfaction, that his desires never degenerate to greed, that he be dignified but without disdain, and that he be commanding but not domineering.'

2. 'What is meant by beneficence without expenditure?' asked Tzŭ Chang. The Master replied: 'To benefit the people by the development of their natural resources; is not this a public benefaction without expense to the revenue? If he select suitable works to exact from them — who then will be dissatisfied? If his desires are for the good of others, and he secure it, how can he be greedy? The wise ruler without considering whether the persons concerned are many or few, or the affair small or great, never permits himself to slight them, — is not this to be dignified without disdain? The wise ruler arrays himself properly in robe and cap, and throws a nobility into his looks, so that men looking upon him in his dignity stand in awe of him, — and is not this commanding without being domineering?'

3. 'What is the meaning of the four bad rules?' asked Tzŭ Chang. The Master replied, 'Putting men to death without having taught them their duty, — which may be called cruelty; expecting the completion of works when no warning has been given, — which may be called oppression; remissness in ordering and then demand for instant performance, — which may be called robbery; and likewise, when giving rewards to men, offering them in grudging fashion, — which may be called being merely an official.'

CHAPTER III

1. The Master said: 'He who does not know the divine law cannot become a noble man. 2. He who does not know the laws of right conduct cannot form his character. 3. He who does not know the force of words, cannot know men.'

INDEX

Note.—The names of the disciples in italics are those most used in *The Analects*.